STYLE

an Anti-Textbook

STYLE
an Anti-Textbook

Second Edition, Revised

Richard A. Lanham

Paul Dry Books
Philadelphia, 2007

First Paul Dry Books Edition, 2007

Paul Dry Books, Inc.
Philadelphia, Pennsylvania
www.pauldrybooks.com

Text type: Minion
Display type: Trade Gothic
Composed by P. M. Gordon Associates
Designed by 21xdesign.com

Printed in the United States of America

Library of Congress Cataloging-in-Publication Data

Lanham, Richard A.
    Style : an anti-textbook / Richard A. Lanham. — 2nd ed., rev.,
1st Paul Dry Books ed.
        p.   cm.
    Revised ed of: 1st ed. New Haven : Yale University Press, 1974.
    Includes bibliographical references.
    ISBN-13: 978-1-58988-032-0 (pbk. : alk. paper)
    ISBN-10: 1-58988-032-3 (pbk. : alk. paper)
    1. English language—Style. 2. Prose literature—Technique.
I. Title.
    PE1421.L3 2007
    808'.042—dc22
                                                      2007013845

ISBN-13: 978-1-58988-032-0
ISBN-10: 1-58988-032-3

Once Again, For Carol

And the things thought essential to a textbook—impersonality, numbered and labeled paragraphs, an obvious style, test questions at the end of the chapter—are they not death? The Dark Ages, it seems, was a time when people read textbooks and thought they were literature.

Charles Horton Cooley, *Life and the Student*

Contents

Origins

It TAKES SOME temerity to publish, in a new edition, a book written more than thirty years ago. It takes even more if, as is the case here, the book argues for pleasure in writing and speech. Pleasure in words does not occupy a dominant place in the contemporary panoply of pleasures. In my own defense, I can say only that I think it should and that my attempts to argue the case in this book are as needed now as they were when I first wrote it. Indeed, were I to write it again, I'd write it just the same way, and so I've left it pretty much as it was. I think the second edition of the book gains strength this way, for readers can judge for themselves whether, in hindsight, its basic arguments remain pertinent and sound. But the discussion does need bringing into the present tense, and I've tried to do this in a series of comments, called "Afterthoughts," which I've appended to each chapter. I've also made a few minor changes, bringing the pronouns into current gender correctness, blunting a few too-sharp expressions, and revising the Bibliographical Note into Notes for Further Reading. In the "Sequels," I treat myself—and I hope the reader— to a few general reflections.

To introduce the book to new readers, though, let me preface it with a couple of stories. They tell you where this book came from, how this particular leopard got its spots.

Story #1. *An offer I had to refuse.*

I WAS SITTING in my office at UCLA one sunny spring day when an unexpected visitor knocked on my door. He was a senior editor of a major composition textbook publisher, and he told me that he had heard I spent a lot of time reading student writing and that I was a demon, if not demonized, commentator thereon. Was this true? I confessed it. Would I then possibly be interested in producing a new edition of this publisher's mainstream Freshman Composition text? Everyone has his price, we're told. I had not thought of what my price might be for such an activity, but it was certainly less than the sum mentioned by the senior editor as a possible reward. My wife and I had just bought a house, a not inconsequential act in Los Angeles. I promised to give the matter serious thought, and I did. I went down the hall to the composition director's office and asked him for an armful of the most popular handbooks (as texts of this sort are usually called), including the one in question.

I read them. I then wrote the senior editor a letter telling him that I could not undertake the work. It was not that I felt it beneath me nor, for certain, that I didn't need the money. It was that I found these books excruciatingly boring. I knew that, as soon as I started work, I would start making jokes and, worse yet, these jokes would reflect my conviction that the theoretical basis of the books was wrong—or, to wrap the matter up more tactfully, seriously incomplete. I couldn't do this job for the same reason I couldn't sing the soprano lead in *La Traviata*. I just didn't have it in me.

My letter, however, was not written in a judicious frame of mind. I waxed satirical and ironical about how and why I thought that these books, which I had come to think of as "The Books," were so misguided and therefore so boring. I made jokes about this. A reply soon arrived. I no longer have it in my files, but in paraphrase it went: "I much enjoyed your letter and passed it around the office and everybody else enjoyed it too. Why don't you write a book like that? We'd like to see it."

That summer, I wrote it and sent it off. It came right back with a reply that I must again give in recollected paraphrase: "We enjoyed your manuscript very much, but we could never publish anything like that! It would offend too many people in the composition world." I then fell back on a friendship and sent it to the director of Yale University Press. Would Yale be interested? They were. One publication committee member remarked, after they had voted thumbs up for publishing it, "It's not a textbook, it's an *anti-textbook*," and that's how this book got its name.

Story #2. "*Look it up in the index to Sister Miriam!*"
IN MY FIRST YEAR of graduate school, I found my professors using Latin and Greek terms I had never heard of to describe verbal patterns. Words like *isocolon* and *zeugma* and *homoioteleuton.* When I asked more seasoned students what these words meant, I was always told, "Look it up in the index to Sister Miriam." This enticing advice pointed toward a book titled *Shakespeare's Use of the Arts of Language,* by Sister Miriam Joseph, C.S.C. It was an eye-opener. Maybe, for me and in retrospect, *the* eye-opener.

What I found there showed me a new way to read Shakespeare, and indeed all of literature. I saw not the customary

Shakespeare of profundities, moral and political, but a Shakespeare infatuated with language and playing wild games with it just for fun, creating characters who would never say "I don't like it" when they could say "It is most retrograde to my desire." Sister Miriam's analysis of Shakespeare's language also planted in my mind, though the tree did not grow until later, a different way to teach prose composition, a way which emphasized pleasure rather than duty, which allowed words to escape from the penalty box and get back to skating. Out of that effort grew the present book.

Los Angeles, 2007

Preface to the First Edition

A WORD ABOUT subject and audience. This book seeks to provide both a preface to the study of prose composition and a context for it. It argues that the premises from which the study of composition now departs—clarity, plainness, sincerity—are incomplete and seriously misleading. It suggests alternative premises and an alternative pedagogy, and is thus about both prose style and the teaching of prose style, addressed to both student and teacher. It also suggests that the study of style has objectives more profound, and more enjoyable, than simply the faithful and useful communication of concepts. It seeks to supply, that is, new purposes for stylistic study as well as new premises.

This is not a textbook, then, but a counterstatement to the textbooks now in use and the widespread attitudes they express. It is neither a practical guide to better prose, a handbook of dos and don'ts, nor a scholarly analysis, historical or schematic, of prose styles. It aims, rather, to provide a framework within which such books can be studied with more profit than they are now.

I have tried to reach not only the classroom but also a general American audience, for the problem extends beyond the classroom to the nation. The specifically American setting is crucial, and nothing but confusion has ever come from ignoring it. America is the only country in the world rich enough to have the leisure, and democratic enough to have the inclination, to teach its whole citizenry not merely to write, but to write well. Time will try the truth of this hopeful enterprise. Meanwhile, such a purpose seems new enough, and daring enough, to require premises, pedagogy, and purposes equally so.

My colleague and friend Alan Roper has given the type-script that kind of critical reading and sympathetic under-standing every author dreams of, especially when his doubts are greatest and his hopes about to expire. I would also like to thank Stanley E. Fish, Ronald Freeman, Mary R. Georges, Ruth M. Holmes, Loren G. Lee, and James Carbone, for help-ful readings and suggestions. And I stand in debt to a yet larger group, my students: those in English 1 and 2, and in the remedial sections, at Dartmouth; those in Composition for High School Teachers, in Advanced Composition, and in English 1 and 2, at UCLA; and those students in my upper division and graduate classes, who did not know they had signed on for a composition class too, but did not resent the addition so much as one might have expected.

I must also acknowledge the help of a sabbatical leave from the University of California, Los Angeles, and a grant from the UCLA Research Committee. This last paid for, if it could not suitably reward, the delightful diligence of my re-search assistant, Elena Barcia. Finally, I must thank the staff of Yale University Press. They have been everything an au-thor could wish his press to be.

R.A.L.
Los Angeles, 1973

1 The Prose Problem and "The Books"

> Your damned nonsense can I stand twice or once, but some-
> times always, my God, never.
>> Svatislav Richter, to the second flute
>> at Covent Garden

PEOPLE HAVE THOUGHT prose style many things—persuasion or mere music, duty or pastime, ornament only, the
man himself. It has been left for Americans to think it a
problem: the National Problem, the Communications Problem. From time to time, we castigate our daily speech, but it
is for written utterance—for prose—that the true jeremiads
are reserved. These are hard to assess. Prophets of doom
rarely confess their prejudices. And for the American prose
scene the prejudices are many, and probably inevitable. As an
English commentator put it: "On subjects like America and
Prose one's mind cannot be made a blank" (Geoffrey Moore,
"American Prose Today," p. 351).

It is easy enough for the language teacher to deliver himself of unarguable pronouncements, especially if these reveal
his calling to be crucial, unvalued, and underpaid. Language
provides the medium of conscious life, and language teachers ought often to point this out. If language becomes truly
unexpressive, we indeed become a mob. With so much at
stake, it should not surprise us that the epithets for current
American prose (and the educational procedures that create
it) are quick to damn. Jacques Barzun's summary phrase
"Black Rot" may stand as example. Yet the world has most

7

often been arthritic in its utterance. Whether our historical situation, our prose problem, emerges as truly more severe than that of other times or other countries, no one, with any hard evidence at least, can at present judge. This problem, like so many of ours, seems unprecedented. No other country has ever considered skill in prose composition essential to good citizenship and has tried to teach this skill to a majority of its citizens. The citizens of no other country have, so far, undergone so heavy a verbal saturation by the media. The scope and magnitude of our problems, their now-or-never fundamentality, vastly increase the pressure on the means—ultimately language—through which they are to be expressed and perhaps solved.

At the same time, our processes of education—and the theories that underlie them—have been undergoing dislocating stresses unequaled in the West since the Reformation. We do not know how much of what we loosely call "communication" is written, how much oral, or what the relationship between the two kinds is. We possess no calculus of misunderstandings. "Failure of communication," our cant term for all occasions, often masks simple vacancy of mind. A student writes on an examination paper, "Abuses in the Church troubled Martin Luther beyond belief." Does the fault lie with language or the mind? We have no way of measuring the efficiency of our schools in teaching good prose, for there are no agreed upon standards of good prose and no standard of teaching accomplishment to measure against.

Furthermore, the problem of prose—so large, so central —introduces fundamental questions. What exactly *is* communication and how does it take place? What do we *mean* by clarity? How may we separate clarity from special interest, from attempts to persuade, or from correctness? Good prose takes time. Is it always worth it? Does clear writing really make for clear thinking? Are the criticisms of modern prose directed at clarity or at elegance? Does elegance, or eloquence, improve the communication of concepts? In an increasingly oral technology, will we need written communication at all? On the electronic screen, will words take second place to images? Finally, if we are in a crisis of utterance, is it *civilization* that is at stake, or only the joy and pleasure that literate people take in language?

The problem of prose, all this is to say, does not at present admit of scientific (quantitative) resolution, or even of scientific address. We do not know even the magnitude of the problem. As a Welfare Department spokesman once eloquently complained, "We're in a position where we're really not sure of what kind of a situation we're in." Humanists will hasten to add that such a problem should not—by its nature, cannot—profitably endure scientific scrutiny. You may agree, but it is hard to find the agreement reassuring. It leaves us in a shady universe of tentative hints and heuristic guesses. One would like to know at least the boundary conditions of the problem. All that we have now is a growing sense of muddled language, public and private, in which "like" appears every third word and everyone says "You know?" but nobody knows.

To so vaguely defined a problem, one can scarcely speak of a coherent national response. But there has been that kind of activity which begins to define a problem, if not to solve it. It has come through the schools and colleges. No one need anatomize again their performance in teaching students how to write. The schools' failures have been inevitable. Teaching grammar and composition takes a great deal of time, time few teachers in America are given. Because of this massive failure, the weight has fallen on that peculiar American institution, the college course in Freshman Composition. To this course, now ten weeks long or, for real depth, a full semester, come the tired, the poor, the huddled students yearning to be freed. Their training and experience vary from weak to nonexistent. The plan is to have them emerge at the end of the course writing prose as limpid as a purling stream and as lean as a greyhound on a diet. The miracle workers who preside over these classrooms of thirty to forty aspirants are usually graduate students. They have seldom been trained to teach prose composition and may not write good prose themselves. They will teach two sections of such a course—in hard times and places, three. They are students themselves, and upon their performance as such depend their higher degree and subsequent escape from teaching Freshman Comp. Yet they are exhorted to give their whole heart to this shortcut to oblivion. But if they are observant, they will harbor little optimism about what, even at best and at full time, they might accomplish in one course.

Consider what they are trying to teach. The usual Freshman Composition course takes as its subject something called (old-fashion) Rhetoric or (new-fashion) Basic Communications Skills. New or old, it is basically the medieval trivium, or first arts course, a progress of grammar, logic, and rhetoric. The medieval student spent *all* his time on these three *until he got his B.A.* Students now get ten weeks. Invariably, these students know nothing of logic when they begin, practically nothing of grammar, and often literally do not know what rhetoric is. They do know that the course is unimportant to their future academic careers. No professor, if they go into science, will expect them to write comprehensible prose, or penalize—and correct—them if they do not. If they go on to study social science, they will find the lucid prose their eager teaching assistant urges upon them a positive handicap. And even should they remain in the English department, the chance of their being held to a standard of good prose grows daily smaller.

There are more lurid colors for the vignette. Add that the instructors may not know the rules of formal logic themselves, or the modern thinking that has almost transformed the traditional subject. More importantly, they will be aware that in our time there are two "grammars," one traditional and prescriptive, one usage-centered and "transformational." Though they try to explain the same phenomena, the two stand poles apart. Each Freshman Composition class, depending on the text used and the instructor's knowledge and predilection, will offer a different mixture of the two. To so promising a pedagogical situation, add other influences. The Freshman Composition course is formally required of, and thus resented by, all. In an age of few requirements, and those dwindling, it allegorizes cruel and unnatural punishment. Furthermore, the brightest students are often excused from it on the basis of their high-school performance. The rest feel themselves, not without reason, the Awkward Squad.

What is likely to be learned in such a course? In recent years some faculties, answering sensibly "Nothing at all," have abolished it. Nothing is offered in its place. Instead, a spontaneous game of "Let's Pretend" begins, and the students' ineptitude is simply ignored. The problem that high schools gave up on and left to the colleges, the colleges now give up on and leave to the graduate schools and society at large. Even were the class to succeed, grounds for abolition might obtain. The amount of attention paid to changes in student writing ability over the undergraduate years is shockingly small. One excellent study, Albert R. Kitzhaber's *Themes, Theories, and Therapy: The Teaching of Writing in College*, would seem to constitute—though he had not the heart to press his conclusions so far—the best evidence yet for the uselessness of Freshman Composition. Kitzhaber studied Dartmouth College students—bright, carefully selected, and very energetically taught writing in the freshman year, for the most part by seasoned, degree-bearing, full-time faculty members. The students improved. But unless they majored in English, by their senior year they were back to square one. The students worked hard. The instructors worked even harder, graded ten to twenty thousand words a week of undergraduate writing, in detail, revisions submitted—the lot. Yet very little took, very little lasted. Even under optimal circumstances the course failed.

What has gone wrong? It would be comforting to think this failure only one of will and money. If Americans were willing to spend the truly vast sums needed for good schools, the schools themselves would solve the problem. If only the colleges had the money, in their hecatombs of English 1 sections they could solve it. The profession could see the problem, and bracing itself to its duty, do it. Yet even were this battalion of blessings to descend upon us, the problem would remain. Poverties of attitude, not only of funds, create it.

"It is the thought that really matters." This illusion runs deep in American society. When American students sit down, having—sacred thing—"expressed themselves," and are required to revise what they have written, they feel—there is no other word for it—silly. Only a child would do this. What's the point in spending a lot of time prettying things up? The thought is what counts. Style is for English teachers and editors. To be interested in it, especially for a man, is like being interested in furnishing his house—women's work. So, should a student, by guess or by God, actually learn something about prose style, he will find nobody in the society he speedily joins who knows or cares what good prose is, and nothing that encourages him to write well or rewards him if he does. The stupidest and most recalcitrant students of composition usually make the most sensible comment on the course: "Why should I care how I write when nobody else does?"

They are even more right than they know. They point to the joyous world beyond the confines of school and college, but few within the ivory tower know or care either. Professor Kitzhaber puts it fairly:

> The only solution is a general conviction among students that good writing and good thinking are inseparable and that both are characteristic of a liberally educated adult. But students are not likely to develop this conviction as long as their other teachers in school and college so often reveal that they themselves lack it. (pp. 119–20)

Criticizing prose style takes more than knowledge and experience. It takes time. The high-school teacher perhaps does not have the knowledge, and certainly not the time, to develop the experience. As a result, students are sent to college who simply have never thought about prose style. And these students meet a professor who takes his delight in teaching and researching a *subject,* and that subject is seldom prose style. Thus the university, after the genuflection of Freshman Composition, ignores the problem as completely as does outside society.

Good prose does not come from a one-time inoculation. It has to be sustained by the standards of a society, by that society's sense of style. It has to be encouraged, appreciated, rewarded. Its countervailing ugliness has to be mocked. None of this now happens in America. There may once have been enclaves in English departments that did these things. No more. Seldom do we experience good prose in our daily life or try to write it. We are never encouraged to pay attention to language.

It is precisely this act of attention to the verbal surface that American students find so awkward, so artificial, in prose-style instruction. If you ask American students to read a prose passage out loud, they sit paralyzed with fright. It is not simply that they have never in their lives read one aloud, though this is often true. It is that they must pay attention to words in a new way, and they find this acutely uncomfortable. Americans use their language, spoken as well as written, in a chronic absence of mind, like. The result, as the following pages demonstrate, is writing not so much incorrect or unclear—though it is usually both—as simply unseeing.

Our society, then, offers no positive reinforcement to good prose, no negative to bad. Still worse, it offers positive reinforcement to the bad, negative to the good. The media, as one would expect, reflect and exacerbate the American attitude toward language. Words are to use. Advertising, in supplying plastic soul to the media, literally *uses up* words for profit. It parodies divinity in turning the word into matter, into goods. Every day of his life, an American encounters the word primarily in someone's effort to sell him something. He must train himself to look through the word to the trap beneath. Enjoy the language and they've got you. Karl Shapiro called advertising the poetry of the poor. It is the poetry of us all—a poetry that travesties poetry, where the words never exist for themselves, where their dignity, shape, form is never respected, where they are perpetually for sale. Advertising is America's real composition class, its real training in prose style. Faced with advertising, the dedicated teacher of prose composition is like the saintly fireman in the cliché, charging hell with a bucket of ice water.

It is instructive to compare the English with the American tradition of thinking about prose style. The British tradition has been a strongly normative one, but unstated. Good prose, in a common phrase, is like good manners. Everyone may be expected to recognize it and use it without fuss. The rich literary tradition underlying any kind of sensitivity to prose style is likewise assumed. Thus, if you pick up one of the standard discussions of prose written in Britain (see Read, Murry, Sutherland, and Lucas in my Notes for Further Reading), you find that it draws continually on—and supposes familiarity with—the whole range of English literature, and often Continental texts as well. Only with such a grounding can a prose style in English really be understood, be experienced.

Prose may be a "problem" for us as it has never been for the English, precisely because we lack both the literary and the social norms that give it meaning. We can assume neither a norm of gentility nor a literary tradition. Teachers of prose in America are often at a loss when asked to recommend studies of style. Such studies almost invariably talk about it in terms of texts the student has never heard of. One British theorist recommends, as a useful means for testing conciseness in English prose, quick translation into Latin or Greek. Americans, students or not, live in a different world. We are trying to learn something about prose style without the whole context that has, traditionally at least, rendered prose style comprehensible and given it meaning. We are trying to learn in a vacuum. And we may, of course, add as a footnote to the contemporary scene the much-heralded demise of the book. Americans used to read only current fiction. Now they read nothing at all. For written utterance, they have as context only journalism. How accurate such prophecies of doom really are, I suppose few would want to say. But the teacher of composition, at whatever level, will speedily be reminded that she is, more and more, trying to teach prose to people who, at least voluntarily, seldom read *anything*.

A comment by a British translator about American translations points shrewdly to our central difficulty:

> In their own tongue Americans fear no obscurity, no imprecision. When it comes to rendering a foreign page into American English they are hampered, however, by a puritan distrust

for words. Normal Americans have a very small vocabulary. They feel towards words as they feel towards the parts of a car: let them function; no more is asked of them. (Alan Pryce-Jones, "Translations and the Americans")

"They feel towards words as they feel towards the parts of a car." This attitude underlies the prose problem in America. We *use* words but we don't really *like* them. Such an attitude is implicit not only in courses in composition but in the society as a whole. The assumption is Jeffersonian. The best prose style is the one that styles the least. In the best of all possible worlds, there would not be any words at all to mislead, only concepts. In a throwaway culture, words, like everything else, are to be got rid of. If, as I argue here, prose style begins in pleasure and not in clarity, the throwaway assumption defeats us before we begin.

American pragmatism insists that words are for use, not enjoyment; American Puritanism insists that expression is a duty, not a pleasure. We dislike learning foreign languages because such learning requires taking pleasure in words for themselves. Let all the world learn one language (English, lucky for us) so that we can do away with verbal misunderstandings and get down to brass tacks. We learn to speed-read our own language for the same reason. Such an attitude becomes a self-fulfilling prophecy. Prose written without joy can only be read in the same spirit. Given the average quality of American prose, speed-reading it out of existence is probably the best thing. So we come to hate the word, and use it still more ineffectively. "No profit goes where is no pleasure ta'en."

Just as our scientific attempts to "conquer" nature end by destroying and dehumanizing it, our efforts to Do our Duty as Effective Communicators end up holding language at arm's length. We pare away all sense of verbal play, of self-satisfying joy in language, and then wonder why American students have a motivation problem and don't want to write. A literate, reading culture imbibes its joy in language naturally, through its literary experiences. Poetry is, after all, language in a state of play. No readers we, denied this source of joy we then devise a pedagogy that denies every other source as well. We want to degrade all verbal pleasure into utility, just as we degrade all human motive into the cash nexus. And the utilitarian premise, simplified as it is, yet proves false. Good prose no more makes a man thrive in the world than does higher education as a whole. Look at the rich and the famous. John Jay Chapman said all this long ago:

> Now, the truth is that the higher education does not advance a man's personal interests except under special circumstances. What it gives a man is the power of expression; but the ability to express himself has kept many a man poor. (*Learning and Other Essays,* p. 331)

Articulate speech can get you in trouble. Conversely, if you really are great with child to speak, you can get the message across, as did Richter to the second flute at Covent Garden, without speaking the language at all. So instruction in composition builds on a single premise—clarity—and that premise is false.

The simplifications of Freshman Composition are, then, the simplifications of American life. America has faced the prose problem with a characteristically confident attitude, intensely practical on the one hand and high-mindedly moralistic on the other. As a practical matter, we need as much prose style as will get the world's business done expeditiously—a philosophy of denotative clarity—and are willing to pay for only this much and no more. On the other hand, civilization does depend on the state of our native language, and so our approach to the problem of prose style must be unremittingly moral. A typically American commandment is thus precipitated out: Thou shalt be as clear as necessary in order that the world's business be done efficiently and civilization thereby preserved. A broad justification, then, for a narrow theory of prose style. Upon this disjunctive and sometimes contradictory yoking of use and morality has been built the prose pedagogy of America.

We concentrate on utility at the expense of *joie de vivre.* And we then wonder, as de Tocqueville prophesied we would, why life has lost its savor. We rediscover, in fact, the utilitarian value of pleasure. We have begun to do this in American life, perhaps, but not in teaching prose style. A voice from the rigorous past:

> So delicate are the adjustments of thought and language, so many and diverse the differences in the unknown and unnumbered persons we would reach, so great the chances of failure and so slender the assurance of success, that we need a more rigorous devotion, a stricter purpose: to speak and write not merely so as to be understandable, but so as to be *unmistakable.* Nothing less stern will pull our slackness up to exactitude and make our slouching erect and vertebrate. (H. Robinson Shipherd, *The Fine Art of Writing,* pp. 13–14)

This pompous moralism still prevails. Surely we ought to move in the opposite direction from such moral earnestness, stressing not words as duty but words as play. Our efforts to cope with the National Prose Problem might more avail, be finally more utilitarian, if they were willing to embrace a purpose richer and more humane than joyless—and useless— utility. Our national efforts may lack not so much money as imagination. "Speech in its essence," Kenneth Burke tells us, "is not neutral" (*Permanence and Change*, p. 176); it is full of feeling, attitude, emotion. Drain this out in the name of useful unmistakability and you end up with composition-class prose, a dismal grayness which, like so much of American life, seems significant only of its own insignificance. And the spirit of play, the spontaneous joy in words, banished from the front door, will only, as we shall later see, sneak in through the back.

The fundamental problems of prose in America, then, are social as well as pedagogical. How might the study of style best address them? Such study has always been cursed by two perplexities. A course in writing has no immediate context—it is not writing *for* anything—and it has no *subject*. What do you write *about*? Until prose style concerns everyone, and not just English departments, the first question can find only incomplete answers. Students will remain flaccid and unmotivated until some connection is made between writing and the motives their culture really honors. Perhaps the best way to insure "A" papers would be to pay a cash reward. Until we attain that golden sequel, surely what is called for is a theory of prose composition which stresses its pleasures as well as its duties, and supplies some kind of context for these pleasures.

To answer this second question—What do you write about?—generations of impecunious pedagogues have racked their brains. Look-in-your-heart-and-write Sincerity ("My Most Exciting Day at The Beach," "What God Really Means to Me"), Current Events ("Rotten Senator X," "The Slanted Prose of Magazine Y," "The Heartrending Pickle of Minority Z"), Still Life ("A Rhododendron in the Rain")—the search for novelty has been desperate. Surely the question permits a simpler answer.

There is only one inevitable *subject* for a course in writing, writing itself—style. Paul Roberts has thought the great contribution of linguistics to writing instruction to be that linguistics itself becomes the subject ("The Relation of Linguistics to the Teaching of English"). A sampling of the crabgrass prose of linguists scarcely gets our hopes up. Worse, the scientific set of linguistics moves the student in precisely the wrong direction. She should be looking *at* the stylistic surface; instead, she is continually invited to look *through* it to a deep structure beneath. She is encouraged, again, to attend not to style but to something beyond it.

Any writing course in America today should aim at an acute self-consciousness about style. For this purpose, style itself must be the object of contemplation. Writing courses usually stress, not style, but rhetoric's other two traditional parts, finding arguments and arranging them. Yet both, implicit in a study of style, emerge naturally only from a concentration on it. If a student really cannot think logically to begin with, he needs another course. Writing prose will be beyond him. Composition should not be asked to do too much. Its natural subject is style.

Composition texts have not seen it this way. They stand foursquare on the trivium. In fact, they try to include everything. General Acceptability lies heavy upon them. The publishers, to ensure big sales, have them certified ninny-proof by boards of special advisers. Perhaps this is why most of them bore us so. They have a special tone, the tone you use to a child old enough to understand but who doesn't. Big, heavy, textbooky, with endpaper polychrome charts, they make the heart sink just to look at them. They have been variously traduced as fast-buck work, but this gives a false impression. They seem nothing if not laborious. They aim to take in a typical freshman, gawky and clueless, process him cover to cover, and turn out a conflation of Walter Pater and George Orwell. No questions have been spared, no exhortations finessed, no error uncatalogued or unabbreviated into a superefficient squirrel chatter of *uncs, orgs, parals,* and *logs.* No, it is not earnestness that composition texts lack. It is joy. Their earnestness lies upon the spirit like wet cardboard. The moral imperative above all characterizes these texts, a bizarre class of endeavor which, as I made my way through them, spontaneously christened themselves "The Books."

Good prose, The Books tell us, is a duty. Their conception of prose is utilitarian and moral. If language is the means of conscious life, then Good Prose, like Cleanliness, must stand next to Godliness. This perpetual moralizing about language haunts all modern writing about style. So

Aldous Huxley, that new-model Sunday-school teacher and papier-mâché sage, on *Words and their Meanings:*

> When Gotama insisted on Right Speech, when Jesus stressed the significance of every idle word, they were not lecturing on the theory of semiosis; they were inculcating the practice of the highest virtues. Words and the meanings of words are not matters merely for the academic amusement of linguists and logicians, or for the aesthetic delight of poets; they are matters of the profoundest ethical significance to every human being. (p. 28)

Perhaps it was his American audience (a Los Angeles audience, as you can tell—Buddha is addressed by his familiar name) that prompted Huxley to such sobriety. Because Americans do not think words important at all, writers about words must call them vital. Thus in The Books, in most writing about style, the imperative mood prevails. Here is a list of exhortative chapter headings from one of The Books:

Do not take yourself too seriously
Consider your readers
Make your writing talk
Be a good mechanic
Sharpen your thesis
Believe in your thesis
Build your essay in three parts

What can you say? What can you ever say to Polonius? A student, if he is on scholarship or has an ambitious mother, may actually try to earn all these merit badges. But if he has any spirit, he'll murmur a well-chosen four-letter word and go out and get stoned. Or if he is exceptionally thoughtful, he may explore the contradictions embedded in these commandments:

> What is "too seriously"? Why *three* parts? How can I believe in a thesis obviously hoked up for English 1? Write from a suitable design? You might as well say "Be intelligent." In fact that's what all The Books' mottoes come down to, isn't it? Why not just pass out wall plaques reading "Don't Screw It Up Again!"

Students of style are bombarded with self-canceling clichés. Here's a quintessence taken from The Books published in the last hundred years:

> Be plain; Avoid "fine writing"
> Avoid bluntness; Articulate your sentences gracefully
> Make your writing spontaneous
> Revise!
> Be yourself
> Imitate the masters
> Write from your own experience
> Read widely ("A man will turn over half a library to make one book," Samuel Johnson is repeatedly quoted as saying)
> Make an outline
> Don't over-outline
> Be serious without being stuffy
> Study spoken speech
> Writing and Speaking are different things
> What the prose writer needs is a temperament nicely balanced between the sprightly and the phlegmatic, a lively mind and a deliberate judgment. His ideas will flow easily, but not too impetuously.

And, on a larger scale, Dickens and Buffon advise that writing talent is an infinite capacity for taking pains. Edward S. Martin disagrees: "I don't think writing can be taught much beyond the rudiments. The rest of it seems to come from the teacher who runs the singing classes for the birds." All this advice, totaled up, yields "Nothing succeeds like success." "Success," of course, is never specifically defined. Sir Herbert Read, in *English Prose Style,* writes:

> But is there an abstract entity, an absolute or "pure" style, to which all styles approximate, or against which all styles are judged? I think there probably is, but it follows from my definition of prose that such a style can never be defined. (p. xii)

This difficulty doesn't bother Sir Herbert as much as it ought to. For it exposes what we might call the Fallacy of Normative Prose. All prose style cherishes a single goal, and that goal is to disappear. The aim is the same for all: clarity, denotation, conceptual fidelity. The imperative of imperatives in The Books is "Be clear." The best style is the never-noticed. Ideally, prose style should, like the state under Marxism, wither away, leaving the plain facts shining unto themselves.

One of the difficulties Freshman Composition has faced, then, though The Books take no notice of it, is trying to teach the invisible, to discuss something that, ideally, isn't there at all. In a real and literal sense, The Books have argued their subject out of existence. They do not teach style, they abolish it. And it is around this fascinating vacuum that the American fetish for correctness, the agony over those droll Victorian antimacassars "usage" and "abusage," so resolutely assembles.

Anyone who dips into The Books soon sees that their advice runs to a dreary sameness. Yet successful prose styles vary as widely as the earth. A hundred different styles cannot be accurately described by a single set of apothegms, eulogistic or dyslogistic. That the transparent prose norm, that reified nonentity Expository Prose, leaves out all prose fiction and nine-tenths of nonfiction prose ought at least to have *troubled* someone. People seldom write simply to be clear. They have designs on their fellow men. Pure prose is as rare as pure virtue, and for the same reasons. The classical discussions of style concern themselves less with clarity than with more common human purposes, with advantage and pleasure. But The Books, written for a world as yet unfallen, depict a ludicrous process like this: "I have an idea. I want to present this as a gift to my fellow human beings. I fix this thought clearly in mind. I follow the rules. Out comes a prose that gift-wraps thought in transparent paper." If this sounds like a travesty, it's because it is one. Yet it dominates prose instruction in America. Prose composition masquerades as a one-step operation that aims to communicate concepts.

The Books seldom tantalize themselves with large hopes, but let us imagine their dream world come true. A world neither too short nor too long, neither formal nor familiar, impersonal nor idiosyncratic, neither too spontaneous nor too carefully revised. A bore. Such a world would be as tedious as the heavenly paradise on which it is so embarrassingly modeled. Talleyrand, an expert at living in the fallen world, thought language was invented so that man could *conceal* what he really thinks. This Kierkegaard improved to "so that he can hide the fact that he doesn't think at all." Both come closer to the truth than The Books' simplistic paradigm.

The American blindness to style is intensified by such a paradigm. Once again, down with words and up with ideas. The Books march off dutifully to precisely the wrong battle. The pedagogy of style in America ought to *contradict* this fixation, not reinforce it. Such a strategy will be simplistic, but in the opposite direction. The prevailing wind bloweth toward meaning, toward concept on the one hand and morality on the other; let us blow toward style, verbal pattern. Such a procedure involves an exaggeration, but one more faithful to the real nature of prose. The Books, when they teach clarity as be-all and end-all, teach an extravagant simplification, a simplification that students often sense though seldom articulate.

I propose an alternative goal: not clarity, but a self-conscious pleasure in words. Such self-consciousness is the only stylistic attitude likely to last beyond the classroom. The only prose didacticism likely to work in America is autodidacticism, and the only possible basis for such teaching is an acute awareness of stylistic surface. Everything in a composition course should be directed toward such an aim. Not clarity, but attention must come first. Only such a therapy will compensate for the literary tradition that even literate Americans do not possess. Only such an emphasis will aerate the vacuum of stylelessness into which prose-style teaching evaporates, will provide the reinforcement that society fails to offer. Only such self-consciousness will equip Americans to cope with the verbiage that surrounds them, to banquet off the nonsense.

What we have now is a tedious, repetitive, unoriginal body of dogma—clarity, sincerity, plainness, duty—tarted up every week in a new, disposable paperback dress. The dogma of clarity, as we shall see, is based on a false theory of knowledge; its scorn of ornament, on a misleading taxonomy of style; the frequent exhortations to sincerity, on a naïve theory of the self; and the unctuous moralizing, on a Boy Scout didacticism. Instruction in style ought to concentrate on what can be taught. Goethe, in his conversations with Eckermann, is reputed to have said that "if any man would write in a noble style let him first possess a noble soul." Wonderful, but not much help. It may be, though some wise men have denied it, that virtue can be taught, but it seems unlikely that it can be taught in Freshman Composition. Nor sincerity. Nor spontaneity. Nor true grit. What can be taught is words. And they must be taught in the full matrix of human utterance, written and spoken, accompanied by a theory of style equally broad. A student bright enough to be taught style needs a context for it beyond didactic precept, an intelligible and sound context. Style cannot be taught only by lists of self-contradicting proverbs, strings of dos and don'ts. Students so instructed are not being taught; they are being housebroken.

I recommend, in what follows, a particular strategy for a particular time and place. Prose style cannot be taught, as it has been, in—and as—a vacuum. It will simply end up, as has been happening with increasing frequency (vacuums being hard to teach), not being taught at all. It cannot be taught as a duty, for you cannot teach as duty what society does not feel a duty. Style must be taught for and as what it is—a pleasure, a grace, a joy, a delight. Pleasure will not, it is true, teach the dumb to speak, the stupid to write, or the bad to practice goodness. But neither will anything else.

Afterthoughts

Much has changed since these words were written, but more has not. The changes first.

The word moves from page to screen.   In 1974, the first personal computer was still two years in the future, and when it came it was a primitive device. As late as 1979, when my Writing Programs office bought its first word-processor, it did nothing but process words in obvious ways, but it cost $15,000 and was as big as a refrigerator. Now we text-message on a cell phone smaller than the wax tablet Roman schoolboys used as a notebook. Words on a screen work in a volatile medium unlike the fixity of print. Readers can write back, turning a one-way communication into the present walkie-talkie world. As part of this migration, words have ceded part of their communicative territory to images, and to new mixtures of words and images.

Secondary orality.   In a landmark of literary scholarship, Milman Parry reinterpreted the poems of Homer as emerging from an *oral* culture, a culture without writing. The wisdom of such a culture must be preserved in conversation, memorized legend, and poetic performances. Later, after the Greeks adopted and adapted the Phoenician alphabet, this memorized cultural information was written down and became "literature." Oral poetry depended on memorized oral formulae and a series of standard rhythmic patterns, and these remained as an oral ingredient in written literature.

In a lifetime of reinterpretive thinking, Father Walter Ong made clear how strong these oral remnants were. We live, he argued, in a period of "secondary orality," a time when the habits of orality remain but are very differently employed because the fundamental cultural records are kept in written form. Never has a scholarly thesis been more confirmed by circumstance. Every person sitting, walking, driving with a cell phone glued to one ear proves the case. People want, if they can, to be continually talking to one another, just as oral cultures do. But there are other indications, of course: talk radio, and the resurrection of radio itself; cheap, increasingly free, internet telephony; talk shows on TV, audio books, etc. The cultural conversation has become once again a real conversation, rather than one carried on in print. We even have a proliferation of public wise persons, a job category popular in oral cultures. In oral cultures, orators tend to be long-winded because when the talking stops the information fades away. You'd think that in the age of sound bites, such prolixity would fade away, but it has returned in endless repetition of the same information. The flow of TV wisdom reminds you of the all-afternoon harangues with which Fidel Castro used to favor us.

A secondary orality such as the last quarter century has brought mixes the spoken and the written word in endlessly new combinations. This mixture of spoken and written affects the teaching of writing, and speaking, just as much as the new mixture of word and image. Written prose has regained its voice.

The great feast of languages.   The mixture, strong enough even when I wrote, continues to churn between two poles.

On the one hand, English marches ever forward as a world language. On the other, never have there been such language mixtures as now. On a walk in London or Los Angeles you may well hear many languages without any of them being English. How do you teach English composition in a school where announcements are regularly made in English, Spanish, Vietnamese, and Farsi? Where students may speak at home any of a dozen other languages? The traditional standards of English teaching, what used to be called "genteel correctness," have been under attack in the last quarter century as—that word of ultimate opprobrium—"elitist." But in our present polyglot orality the problem runs much deeper. What happens to the literary standard, the pattern of literary reading, which stands behind such genteel correctness when a Los Angeles housepainter from Guatemala, illegal but ambitious, goes to his night class in English after a hard day on the ladder and the freeway? What kind of "correctness" does he need? He, and many like him, are trapped between the two poles of the great feast, English on the one hand, the multilingual mix on the other. Teaching English as a second language may have become more important than teaching it as a first.

Professionalization. More parochial changes have supervened in the last quarter century as well. The teaching of composition has become a more clearly defined professional specialization, and has gained more support and recognition. Many talented people work within it, and the phenomenal dedication, and sense of its importance, which writing teachers have always brought to their task, burns as bright as ever. Nowhere in the educational spectrum, I would submit, does one find more dedication to the task in hand.

Plagiarism. The ugliest change in the intervening years must be the enormous growth in plagiarism. It has several causes: Electronic display makes it so easy; increasing pressures to write—and this operates at the scholarly top as well as the student bottom of the educational ladder—encourage cheating; many different kinds of students are being asked to perform tasks new to them, and the tasks themselves are often ill-defined; student papers are often read perfunctorily and, in return, students write them in the same spirit. I myself see moral decay as part of the mixture, a decay which has undermined the basic seriousness.

Now on to what has *not* changed.

The prose problem persists. Here's a headline from the *Wall Street Journal*'s Web site *CareerJournal.com:* "M.B.A. Recruiters' No. 1 Pet Peeve: Poor Writing and Speaking Skills." The article begins, "For Chris Aisenbrey, director of global university relations at Whirlpool Corp., it's a daunting challenge these days to hire literate M.B A. students who can write a coherent letter or memo. Too often, what he gets from job applicants are collections of rambling thoughts littered with misspellings and grammatical gaffes" (01/17/2006). He goes on: "It is staggering, the frequency of typos, grammatical errors and poorly constructed thoughts we see in emails that serve as letters of introduction." Such complaints are commonplace, and at all levels. I have just reviewed the changed circumstances that have made the problem worse. Certainly nothing, in the educational system or elsewhere, has made it any better.

Writing instruction is, as it was when I first wrote this book, something which all agree should be done, which some are willing to pay others to do, but which very few will do themselves. Why is this? I talk in this chapter about the fundamental conviction that "it is the thought that really matters." This conviction continues to thrive, unconsidered and unimpaired.

The *CareerJournal.com* article illustrates the problem perfectly when it continues: "Recruiters say they can count on students from any of the major business schools to bring solid knowledge of accounting, marketing, strategy and other business fundamentals. What distinguishes the most sought-after schools and M.B.A. graduates are the 'soft skills' of communication and leadership that happen to be among the hardest to teach." The fundamental things in business are accounting and marketing. They are the "hard skills." Communication, writing, and speaking, are for the softies.

"Hard" and "soft" are loaded words. Doesn't anybody ever think about what this terminological bias implies in the modern world of business? What is marketing, at its heart, but persuasion, a modern subset of classical rhetoric, that most ancient of soft skills? What is the "brand"—that central, that hardest of hard business concepts—but applied poetry, that soft skill for professional wimps? Just think of the costs—hard cash costs—that the professional accounting world has incurred because it allowed its information channels to be radically polluted.

And consider this proposition: Writing and speaking are among the hardest to teach. What nonsense! True it is that they require work, but that is because few people, outside composition programs, are willing or able to take the time to teach about words, how they work, the patterns they fall into, the energy they should convey. And so the puzzlement, igno-rance, and incompetence float ever upward from elementary school to business school. But the educational tradition about how to teach speaking and writing is two-and-a-half thousand years old. A good deal has been learned in that time. Are we really to believe that, compared to learning what used to be called the "trivium," the basic package of gram-mar, logic, and rhetoric, teaching about how to package de-rivatives or securitize complex real estate deals is a piece of cake? It is not that we don't know how to do it; it is that most teachers won't do it. We really still don't believe, in spite of all The Books' pious exclamations, that it is worth doing. And we won't pause to ponder why we don't. We confront a studied disinclination to use the mental equipment.

The problem has gotten deeper since I wrote, for another and more profound reason. In the last half-century, we have mutated from an economy based on physical stuff you dug out of the ground and shaped into use to an economy based on human attention. This change is not hard to see. We all know by now that the economy has moved from physical stuff to information, the codes that form and control the stuff. (I've written about this change in *The Economics of Attention*. See the Notes for Further Reading.) We live in an information economy. Economics, in its usual definition, is the science that studies the allocation of scarce commodities. But infor-mation is not scarce. We're drowning in it. What *is* scarce is the human attention needed to make sense of it. How you attract and direct human attention is not one of the "hard" skills, like accounting. It is a softy. It is all about persuasion. And the "art of persuasion" has been the usual definition of rhetoric, of all those softy communication skills. Business schools, schools in general, will soon have to notice that, in an attention economy, the "hard" and the "soft" skills change places. The really vital skills in "brand engineering" are communications skills.

If the business schools have not noticed this momentous shift of emphasis, neither have the colleges and universities. Composition instruction is, indeed, more generously supported than it used to be. This is great news. But, from all that I can determine, this new specialization has chosen to emphasize political allegory, not prose style. Courses in prose style, either in English departments or composition programs, lie very thin on the ground. Here too, words don't really matter; it is the message—in this context the political lessons—that matters.

It is more important than ever, then, that we have an adequate, a comprehensive, theory of prose style. The plea I made in this chapter needs to be made again, and louder. More than ever, we need "a particular strategy for a particular place and time," and this strategy must take into account a new kind of economy, a boiling linguistic mixture, a movement from page to screen as profound as the invention of printing, a secondary orality which has grown cell phones out of people's ears. How to do this is not altogether clear, but I'm sticking with the basic argument of this chapter. It must be *style* that we teach, and it should be taught as a pleasure, a grace, a joy, a delight.

I came down hard on advertising in this chapter. I wouldn't do that now. Advertising works in ways far more complex than I was then willing to concede or, indeed, able to understand. Nor is the matter of who reads what nearly so clear as I made it out to be. The situation today is even cloudier. On the one hand, we have surveys that say the average American reads one book a year and that half the books printed in the United States are pulped unread. On the other hand, we have Rowling's Harry Potter tales and O'Brian's Captain Aubrey and Dr. Maturin sea stories, books that have created immense and diverse audiences. And, as a final *mea culpa*, I retract the sophomoric remark about the gray insignificance of American life. What a stupid thing to say!

2 The Uses of Obscurity

Dic, aliquem sodes hic, Quintiliane, colorem. haeremus.
[Quick, Quintilian, an excuse, for Heaven's sake. I'm stuck.]
Juvenal 6.280–281

"D'ABORD LA CLARTÉ," Anatole France exhorts us, "puis en-core la clarté, et enfin la clarté"—clarity first, last, and always. No one has ever disagreed. "Prose," John Middleton Murry tells us in *The Problem of Style*, "is the language of exact think-ing; it was made for the purpose; and I suppose that a prop-osition in Euclid is an elementary example of good style, though in an absolutely noncreative kind" (p. 52). The Books build upon clarity as upon a rock. Good prose stands like a well-washed window giving onto the Kingdom of Thought. So James Sutherland argues in *On English Prose:* "It is good prose when it allows the writer's meaning to come through with the least possible loss of significance and nuance, as a landscape is seen through a clear window" (p. 77). In such a race, either Swift or Dryden usually finishes first, with lesser seventeenth- and eighteenth-century stylists down the field. Before then, since then, and in America of course always, it has been downhill. Such a style, as Sutherland continues, "was too good to last."

Scholars have the right, of course, to issue prescriptive definitions of anything at all, and certainly of good prose. But as a description of what prose has actually been like and done, this definition ought to strike us as hopelessly inadcquate—preposterous, in fact. It describes with any accuracy the prose of very few writers, and does not really, as we shall see, describe even them. To use Swift as norm or sanction for an everlasting "Be clear" simply leaves most prose out of contention. ("The continued vitality of Swift's style is a great consolation to the theorists," Sir Herbert Read reassures us in *English Prose Style*.)

People, even literary people, seldom content themselves with being clear. They invent jargons, argot, odd ways of being clear. They impose nefarious designs upon their neighbors. They repeat things for the pleasure of repetition. They usually swim in a muddy ineptitude, and even when they succeed in being clear it is often only to seem clever. You would think, from the unexamined god-term Clarity has become, that students of prose had never heard of nonreferential language—emotional, phatic, symbolic, purely social. A wholly denotative prose is found as seldom as a purely denotative poetry. People are just not that way. "Be clear!" The moral version, "Be good!" offers as much help. No one would *disagree,* but such moral coordinates do not describe prose in a fallen world. Clarity stands indeed as a laudable aim. If we are willing to define it broadly enough, it may stand for all laudable aims. But narrow or broad, it needs examination.

The university, you might think, would be the place, if any, to find clarity most in demand, most sought after and applauded. We might, then, apply the clarity touchstone to some typical academic prose. Consider these three examples, selected at reasonable random. (I did select for a student-professor-administrator cross-section.)

A letter from an undergraduate to the student newspaper:

The fall quarter is coming to an end. Although this is not surprising in itself, the "Bell Syndrome" is. Students on this campus must become cognizance [*sic*] of the fact that those students that succumb to the "Bell Syndrome" has facilitated others to escape. Those students which pass a course satisfactorily should be aware that individual achievement alone did not accomplish this. In part, it was accomplished at the expense of other students to the "Bell Syndrome."

Moreover, it should be obvious that one way to increase admissions to the University without necessarily increasing the total population of the University is to enforce the bell shape distribution of grades. This will ultimately take its toll of college students.

The goals of education has become obfuscated at the high school level and this is manifested as high school "drop outs." Likewise at the college level, students that succumb to the "Bell Syndrome" are college "put outs."

The inoculation against the "Bell Syndrome" will necessitate an all out effort on the part of all students to ensure no one falls victim of it.

Tolerance of the "Bell Syndrome" only perpetuate the existing system. Students that confess to greater involvement in the community-at-large are only deluding themselves because of their continued tolerance of the "Bell Syndrome."

Has it not occurred to students that some of the constituents of the community may comprise victims of the "Bell Syndrome" which facilitate a greater chasm in relationship than already exist.

If students cannot relate to other students, how can they relate to the community. Students must not allow the umbra of the "Bell Syndrome" to abort the self-determination of fellow students.

Armed with clarity, we can obviously have a romp in this *hortus deliciarum* of adolescent indignation. The author, we might begin by suggesting, should not be allowed to continue in higher education. A junior, presumably in good standing in—needless to say—the Sociology department, he cannot yet hold subject and verb in agreement ("Tolerance . . . only perpetuate," "the goals . . . has become," "students . . . has facilitated"), does not know noun from adjective ("cognizance" for "cognizant"), has trouble locating the relative pronoun used for people ("those students that," "those students which"), falls victim to the dangling prepositional phrase ("to the Bell Syndrome"), has a weakness for the half-understood word, big or unusual ("obfuscated," "umbra," "comprise," "abort"), and loves to coin terms in the best tradition of social science ("put outs," "Bell Syndrome"). He puts together in fresh combinations words he has often heard but never understood. How, for example, do you facilitate a chasm? If an umbra aborts your self-determination, do you sue? He seems to think, not simply with clichés, but wholly in pre-digested phrases: the idiotic "this is not surprising in itself" in the second line, for example, or "constituents of the community" comprising "victims."

What does such prose reveal? Is clarity the problem? Perhaps because the argument is familiar, I can, except for the penultimate paragraph, follow it with a little work. If grades are assigned on a curve, some will rise because others fall. The student has observed that, though some classes may perform so as to fit the curve naturally, others do not. The student has obviously not said *exactly* what he means—merciful heavens—but he has (all he would doubtless profess to want) "communicated." Why, then, is our response to the letter so prompt? That is, not only a "My God, what prose!" but as Stephen Leacock put it, "Willie is no good. We'll sell him."

First, I suppose, comes skirling, scornful laughter at his elementary mistakes of grammar. This, a social judgment, probably dominates any literate reader's response to the letter. But still more than its mistaken grammar, its ugliness stands out. It is not simply that the writer has no feeling for the shape or rhythm of his sentences. (Paragraph four is a good example of this shapelessness.) They are full of unintended sound patterns, "rel*ate*," "necessit*ate*," "facilit*ate*"; "*c*onstituents of the *c*ommunity may *c*omprise." The writer feels indignant, and indignation demands eloquence. Instead, we see him floundering, dramatizing helpless irritation. The letter is unintentionally expressive. The Books would call the problem clarity, but that doesn't describe it. His prose, just barely an adequate vehicle for his thesis, communicates a great deal besides, and this extra communication undermines the thesis.

In the terms of classical rhetoric, the writer has established a disastrous ethos, or public dramatization of character—what we now call image. This ethos ruins his case. The bell syndrome can't be all bad if it threatens a donkey like him. The student has not failed to communicate; he has communicated too well. "Be clear," in this case, would mean eliminating the unintentional revelation of ignorance and folly. The clarity argument ignores the unfailing expressivity of words. The real error comes in the presentation of the writer's self. And, of course, there is nothing—at least for the present, and in his case probably for the future—that the writer can do about his self. Thus when The Books tell him, "Be clear," they are saying, with the Good Book, with the Gospels, "Be born again." The futility of such advice ought to be more apparent than it is. Such prose as this testifies to problems of training and raw intelligence beyond any power of prose style to cure.

Talking, then, about how the writer communicates a concept leads precisely in the wrong direction here. Dramatization of character demands center stage. If we moralize about what a violation of the sacred-scientific-duty-to-express-concepts-clearly has been committed, we ignore the point and hence fail to help the student—if that is possible. The prophecy of doom will be greeted by the student at all events with an echoing scorn ("Who knows the difference? Who cares?"), which the following selections from his academic superiors do little to dispel.

Consider this memo from a professor:

The Task Force is also concerned that it provide the basis for the faculty of this campus to govern itself, rather than being governed by others less understanding of the nature of the University. Consequently, we are asking you to specify the methods you use to evaluate the effectiveness of your instruction. Likewise, we are seeking your views on the function of evaluation and your suggestions for the implementation of evaluation of instruction on a campus-wide basis. This information will greatly contribute to our recommendations regarding the best possible methods for evaluation of instruction which will at the same time be most acceptable to the greatest number of faculty possible, keeping in mind that diverse forms of evaluation will probably be called for in the face of the diverse functions and characteristics of this institution.

All information will be treated confidentially unless we have your specific permission to reference any of your statements.

This prose is clear enough. The problem is speed. It takes a long time to wade through the bureaucratese. A more accomplished stylist, or someone more impatient to be understood, might have said: "If we don't police the quality of instruction ourselves, someone else will. How do you tell whether you are doing a good job? May we quote you? Your method may be helpful in the tricky job of policing a colleague's teaching." But such a translation into plain English would lose much of what the passage really says. In the student's letter, the range of expressivity outside the boundary of plainness was not intended. No one deliberately proclaims himself an ass. Here, whether the professor intended such a proclamation or not seems unclear. Certainly no one could invent her tin ears deliberately.

Listen to the *sound* of "Likewise, we are seeking your views on the func*tion* of evalua*tion* and your sugges*tions* for the implementa*tion* of evalua*tion* of instruc*tion* on a campus-wide basis." This jangle of "shuns," of like word-endings (in classical rhetorical theory it bore—when intentional—the impressive name of *homoioteleuton*), betrays a person for whom prose has no sound. And, since she never recreates the sound of prose by reading it aloud, her sentences have no shape or rhythm. Such writers often have recourse to endless strings of prepositional phrases that creep like a wounded snake across the page. Try circling the prepositions in the passage. Sentences, for a stylist like this, are likely to be long, labyrinthine, without natural emphasis—so the sentence beginning "This information," which winds its slow length through the second half of the first paragraph. This ineptitude, probably neither a failure to "have something to say" nor "to say it clearly," springs from a deafness to the *sound* of words and a resulting blindness to sentence *shape.* Clarity in the semantic sense, intelligible utterance of concept, does not suffer here. If by clarity we mean euphony, rhythm, syntactical balance, shape, and grace, then we have expanded *clarity* to be synonymous with style.

But a dimension of expressivity inheres in the memo which, though undeclared to the reader, may subconsciously have been intended by the writer. The writer, chairman of a task force, is an aspiring academic bureaucrat. She must sound important, and make her task force sound more so. The plain prose paraphrase I have supplied fails both these purposes. If I say, "Different kinds of teaching are to be judged differently," I am not saying clearly what the professor phrases as "keeping in mind that diverse forms of evaluation will probably be called for in the face of the diverse functions and characteristics of this institution." To the licensed bureaucrat, the plain version seems automatically suspicious. It sounds flip. The writer may not be taking her problem, and above all herself, with sufficient seriousness. Read a little more deeply. Evaluation of teaching is a touchy subject for the faculty. *Anything* you say is going to offend someone. A windy, free-floating verbosity presents itself as the best tactic. "Be clear" is disastrous advice.

Just put yourself in the writer's place. She knows, as does any teacher, that you judge the immediate effect of your instruction by contact with your class. You read their faces, worry about the pace of your lectures, revise them, change the pace in a recitation section, see how the papers and exams go, talk to students. Any teacher involved with her job *knows* how her teaching is going. You can tell that she knows —and how it went—just by looking at her posture after a class. The writer may know this. But she also knows that many of her colleagues are, in the sense of the word *teacher* that this sketch implies, not teachers at all. They do not read their students' papers or tests, see as little of them as possible, do not prepare, much less revise, their lectures, and neither know nor care how well they teach. The writer of the memo knows, as do the receivers of it, that the sudden interest in undergraduate teaching is itself to the last degree hypocritical, and that no one actually expects a colleague to interrupt his research (or lassitude) and dive into teaching. University professors are, however, expected to come up with a bureaucratic gesture ("a fresh evaluation of their teaching") in reply to the Task Force's bureaucratic gesture. That way, everybody is covered. If the student body president complains about poor teaching, he can be "shun"-ted off with evaluations, recommendations, implementations, and new functions for new institutions. These will be welcome to the student body president, of course, because he himself plays apprentice bureaucrat.

The memo, then, given the writer's purpose, succeeds very well. Furthermore, to those who know how to read it, it must seem as clear as day. To complain that the writer uses *reference* as a verb, that she has tin ears, that a sentence for her is a shopping bag she stuffs words into, that she comes across as a pompous humbug—all this misses the point. If she wrote the kind of prose The Books recommend, she would lose her job. Prose style does not work in a vacuum, except in Freshman Composition. It works in a context. The context makes it what it is. If you don't consider context, and often in some detail, you will not understand the prose style. A schoolmarmly "tut, tut" is no substitute for understanding.

If the first passage dramatizes ineptitude, and the second a mixture of ineptitude and intended opacity, the following one seems wholly in the range of intention, a fully self-conscious document of style. A university president writes to his faculty:

> In the face of both the severity and continuing character of the budgetary stringencies which we thus face, we have concluded that we must undertake an immediate and thorough programmatic review and re-ordering of academic priorities—a review that would have been required in any event, although, perhaps, on a less intensive time scale. We are convinced that it is no longer possible to temporize and that action must soon be taken to assure that those elements of our program which are essential to the maintenance of a quality institution are protected and nurtured through consolidation, reduction, and elimination of those other elements which are found upon examination to be inessential or which can be rendered more economical or efficient through organizational or other changes. This process, to be effective, must of course go beyond this Campus to the program of the University as a whole. Indeed, it is increasingly clear that we must press for a prompt re-assessment of the University's Growth Plan in the light of reduced fiscal expectations and seek an appropriate reordering of priorities.
>
> Accordingly, discussions have been initiated with leaders of the Senate, and procedures are being established for the

prompt development and coordinated review of proposals for such changes.

It is anticipated that the formal process will begin within a month, dealing with these aspects of the academic program which at the outset appear to promise most immediate and substantial returns with minimal qualitative loss. It is intended, however, that the process be extended beyond its initial scope through a continuing campus-wide effort at re-evaluation and self-examination. At first these efforts must naturally reflect our reduced budgetary expectations; however, the process is intended to provide an effective means for future planning in anticipation of an eventual return to more nearly adequate levels of support. Indeed, we want, to the extent possible under current time constraints, to identify desirable long-range goals and work back to realistic intermediate positions which will lead to their realization.

Taken in the abstract, in a stylistic universe of grace and elegance, such utterance makes a lover of prose long to slide into a warm bath and open a vein. For it is vintage bureaucratese. Yet, in context, it becomes both comprehensible and, in today's world of hokum, inevitable. The university this president directs had just learned of massive budget cuts—cuts, furthermore, coming for a second successive year after several lean years. Worse still, the cuts included, again for the second year, no raise for the faculty—not even a cost-of-living increase. The faculty, then, the recipients of the letter, were both annoyed and demoralized. What he had to say to them, had he drafted it for a (slightly liberated) Freshman Composition course, would have read like this:

> Look, guys. The campus is broke this year. We've used up our surplus. With the money we've got we can't do everything.

We've got to decide what things we can do well, do them, and stop doing a good many others. We have to plan for the kind of future limited budgets can create.

But how ham-handed, given the bureaucratic situation, such a mode of address would be. If you are telling a man he is going to take a cut in salary, that hard times are here again, you had better be long-winded, dismal, and above all formal. That shows (1) that you *see* the gravity of the situation, (2) that you *feel* the gravity of the situation as he does, (3) that you are the kind of sober and reliable fellow who can *deal with* the situation.

Consider another aspect. What the message really says is that some people are going to be fired ("terminated"), some departments shut down ("phased out"), some administrative kingdoms toppled ("programmatically reviewed"). The whole passage, with this in mind, becomes an elaborate exercise in euphemism. Some, in the event, were actually fooled. But those in danger got the message loud and clear and raised vociferous objections. The prose must be seen as an attempt to forestall such objections, to pretend less stands at stake, above all to project a certain attitude toward what is at stake. The plain-prose mentality would have said to the Speech department, "Look, something's got to go. Much better you than Physics or History." But that is precisely the personality, the ethos, the writer did not want to project. Such utterance would betray both resolution and the settled attitude of a man with personal convictions. As written, we have the fair, aloof, indeed Olympian yet concerned, judgment of a disinterested technocrat. With malice toward none and compassion for all, he grasps the helm and faces the troubled waters ahead. If you find yourself, in the judgment of such a man, "found to be inessential" or "rendered more economical or efficient through organizational or other changes," how can you resent it? Resent *ineluctable economic process*?

We must consider, too, the writer's position. What he has to say is simple to the point of schoolboyishness: "We're broke. We've got to save some money. How to do it?" To which the underpaid professor mumbles, "We need you at $50,000 a year, to tell us this?" A group of students on whom I tried out the reductive paraphrase responded immediately, "He couldn't say that. Sure, it would be clearer, but he wouldn't sound like a college president." Of course not; and so a special language, like unto a royal proclamation, must be devised. Remote, impersonal ("It is intended that" not "I am going to"), euphemistic ("reduced budgetary expectations"), decisive yet not hasty ("We are convinced that it is no longer possible to temporize and that action must soon be taken to assure," rather than "We've got to do something"), the prose style does not seek to be clear but to *define a situation* and a personal role within that situation. In these terms it makes great sense.

And, for those who speak the language, those for whom prose is a problem, an opportunity perhaps, but hardly a pleasure, he spoke crystals of clarity. Watch academic bureaucrats being massaged by such prose. They smile slightly, settle a bit into the awkward lecture-room chairs, the musculature relaxes. They feel at home. The president is being clear. And if he does not Build His Essay in Three Parts or Sharpen His Thesis, no one notices. He has Believed His Thesis and Considered His Readers and all is light.

Clarity (as central normative standard for "good prose") does more harm than good. For clarity is not any single verbal configuration but a relationship between writer and reader. There are all kinds of clarities. The kind The Books build upon, though we may applaud it in an aesthetic vacuum, seldom lives in the world of events, advantage, and pleasure, in the world where most prose lives, moves, has its being. When you say that a prose is clear, you are rewarding success, but the success may be of many kinds, the rewarding for many reasons. Thus the injunction "Be clear!" really amounts to "Succeed!", "Write good prose!", or in cant, "Communicate!" Such advice is bracing but not very helpful. Clarity depends on many things besides an agile syntax, a good ear, and the brevity that sires so much besides wit.

Familiarity, more than any other one thing, would seem to determine clarity. Clarity's model of models, the prose of John Dryden, seems far from clear to a student whose prose reading has started at Thomas Hardy and soared to Ernest Hemingway. Conversely, a psychological report incomprehensible to me opens like a flower to a psychologist. "Translate into English" makes a good classroom rubric for such stuff but would be disastrous put into practice. It would never get published. The journal editor would think it unclear, thin, meager, unprofessional. Familiarity means reassurance. Clarity's first job is to make us feel at home. We want to see where we are. And it is not simple familiarity of manner that we expect, but of content as well. When a politician meets the press, the situation keys us not simply to a manner of answer but a kind of answer. Vague, generalized, evasive, determined—at whatever cost to logic or history—

not to offend, such answers are still "clear" enough in context: "No, I will not be trapped by that vote two years ago," "No, I will not offend Group X." In such a tedious environment only a direct answer (or an indirect question) could really perplex the listener.

Psychologists interested in perception have, ever since the experiments of Adelbert Ames II, known that we tend to perceive what we are predisposed to perceive. This, in turn, is conditioned by what we have already perceived and by the framework we have been taught to perceive in. We don't just see something "out there." Our perceptive apparatus conditions, filters, focuses the raw data that initiate the process of seeing. So it is with prose styles. They are not neutral, dependable, preexistent objects that everyone sees the same way. We must be trained, as Americans for the most part are not, to see them at all. And to see them in the same way (this is what an education in "taste" really means) takes a good deal of training indeed.

Move the argument one step further. Each prose style is itself not only an object seen but a way of seeing, both an intermediate "reality" and a dynamic one. Obviously there can be no single verbal pattern that can be called "clear." All depends on context—social, historical, attitudinal.

Clarity, then, like style in the American architect Thomas Hasting's definition, is "the job done." And it will, in this expanded sense, be achieved only by sensitivity to social situation and verbal surface in their many interrelationships. Exhortation gets you nowhere. When you say "Be clear!" to an indignant adolescent writing a silly letter to a college newspaper which is, if possible, sillier than he, you are really not saying anything about prose. You are saying, "Think straight!" "Try out a little evidence!" "Feel pressures other than those you feel!"—above all, "Grow up!" The prose has indeed revealed these moral inadequacies, but if the moral inadequacies trouble you, address yourself to those and not to the prose. You do not gain the sense of style by being good, working hard, and thinking straight. Verbal awareness, not moral exhortation, finds the way to clarity in prose. America has the exhortation in full supply but hardly the awareness. Perhaps this explains our prose problem.

No absolute norm of "clarity" prevails, then, just as no absolute norm of prose does. No particular choice or configuration of words can pattern perfection. Nor can we judge prose by the scientific precision with which it transmits concepts, since most prose transmits feelings and attitudes, unstated assumptions and embarrassing implications, as well as concepts. When we use words, we use signs. And, as Morse Peckham has pointed out in *Man's Rage For Chaos*, "In examining signs we are perforce within the sign field and cannot get out. Ultimately, to *perceive* is to *choose, will, intend*" (p. 90).

Coleridge defined style as nothing but the clear expression of the meaning. This is fine so long as our definition of clarity and meaning remains broad. Is, then, no prose good or bad but success or failure make it so? The repugnance such a conclusion calls up should reveal more than it has. It means our response is fundamentally aesthetic rather than informational, formal rather than semantic. Good prose, clear prose, is finally an affair of form not of conceptual clarity. It works by pleasing us. As Henri Delacroix says at one point in *Le Langage et La Pensée* (*Language and Thought*): "Le language est jusqu'à un certain point, comme la magie, une technique née du désir, qui assure au désir sa réalisation par des moyens nés du désir." [Language, up to a point, is like magic, a technique engendered by desire, one which assures desire its realization by means born of desire.]

At the base of prose style, then, we find not only the need to communicate but also the spirit of play, the delight in form for its own sake. A zeal to inform has in our time bleached out this delight, but we should not therefore confuse the two. "Prose," one treatise tells us, "has mainly if not entirely a descriptive function." Turn this advice upside down. Description describes only a small part of what prose does. Find its true center of gravity, not in a faithful rendering of Our Inmost Thoughts, or of A Rainy Day at Camp (to borrow from The Books), but in the regularity with which it pleases us. Clarity, like The Books' other shibboleth, persuasion, is not an act of logic but an act of charm.

Let us try to sustain this surprising thesis with examples. Look at a recent model of and monument to clarity, the *New English Bible.* Here, in this new translation, Matthew 7 begins:

> Pass no judgment, and you will not be judged. For as you judge others, so you will yourselves be judged, and whatever measure you deal out to others will be dealt back to you. Why do you look at the speck of sawdust in your brother's eye, with never a thought for the great plank in your own? Or how can you say to your brother, "Let me take the speck out of your eye," when all the time there is that plank in your own? You hypocrite! First take the plank out of your own eye,

and then you will see clearly to take the speck out of your brother's.

Do not give dogs what is holy; do not throw your pearls to the pigs: they will only trample on them, and turn and tear you to pieces.

The new translation's one, indeed only, avowed purpose is clarity. The King James Version (1611) is hard to follow. The most familiar Book has now become the least familiar. The stylistic opacity of Elizabethan English has to be cleared up, along with manifest translational errors of sense and emphasis. In these terms, we applaud. Devout or not, you get the message and get it quick. Sawdust, plank, pigs, you see right through the words to the moral lesson beneath. The King James Version does not do nearly so well:

> Judge not, that ye be not judged. For with what judgment ye judge, ye shall be judged: and with what measure ye mete, it shall be measured to you again. And why beholdest thou the mote that is in thy brother's eye, but considerest not the beam that is in thine own eye? Or how wilt thou say to thy brother, "Let me pull out the mote out of thine eye"; and, behold, a beam is in thine own eye? Thou hypocrite, first cast out the beam out of thine own eye; and then shalt thou see clearly to cast out the mote out of thy brother's eye.
>
> Give not that which is holy unto the dogs, neither cast ye your pearls before swine, lest they trample them under their feet, and turn again and rend you.

Not so clear. "Beam" for "plank," "mote" for "speck," "cast" for "take," "rend" for "tear." The diction perplexes. We raise pigs not swine. Pronoun usage differs. The Elizabethan translation uses a pleonasm "trample them under their feet" which the modern translation cleans up to "trample." Is the modern translation better prose? Better prose for the purpose?

Finally, neither. The *NEB* has purchased its conceptual, or perhaps we should say narrative, clarity at the expense of life and personality. Its prose is committee prose. It has no style. Always clear but never memorable, it fails to please. Why? Its alliteration is unintentional ("pearls . . . pigs," "trample . . . turn . . . tear"); the older version's ("measure . . . mete . . . mote," "beholdest . . . brother's . . . beam") is part of meaning-pattern. The *NEB* translator has, for clarity, avoided pronounced rhythm. Thus the Elizabethan allows himself five "judges" instead of four, makes us see the repetition as a pattern. He carefully repeats the rhythm of "for with what judgment ye judge, ye shall be judged" in the second half of the sentence. The reciprocity he is *talking about* is reflected by the rhythm and syntax of the sentence. He allows himself the negative imperative "Give not" to echo the "Judge not" that begins the passage. The similarity draws the two injunctions closer together as the *NEB* version does not. The syntax of the last sentence is clearer, but at the expense of the climactic structure that lends such stress to *rend* and indeed justifies so strong a word.

The Elizabethan translator has tried, too, to be clear, but natural to the kind of prose he wrote came an effort to please, to please by patterns of sound-arrangement and rhythm. Such devices of the verbal surface may be called ornament, but ornament integral to the prose sense, sense as meaning, entire effect. Is not part of clarity for a holy text its memorability? And does this not inevitably involve sound and rhythm? Church is one of the few places left where prose is read aloud. What we might profanely call the circumstances of performance demand a translation full of the sound and syntax patterns the King James Version supplies naturally because, at that time, prose was still regularly read aloud. The inadvertent alliteration of the *NEB*'s "pearls to the pigs," on the other hand, just makes us giggle.

The pious often object to reading the Bible as literature, preferring to concentrate on what is seriously called "the message." Perhaps we are now in a position to see how mistaken such an objection is. The prose style creates the message, expressing, not merely enhancing, it. Scriptural prose owes fidelity beyond the biblical narrative to the whole of the religious experience. Here the joylessness of the *NEB* renders it—faithful translation as it is—unfaithful to the gospel spirit, deep, rich, rejoicing. The Christ of the *NEB* emerges a clear, cold, lifeless pedant.

Such a comparison as we've made is unfair, of course. The King James Version has been sanctified by time, rendered familiarly central to the Western mind. But isn't this what a religious text should be? You cannot *write* prose thus endowed but, endowment bestowed, it will embody the religious experience more than any new translation ever can. As a scripture, it will inevitably be clearer. Conversely, you can write a prose, flat, lifeless, neutral, scientifically clear, which *can never be remembered.* This is what the *NEB* translators have created. "Clarity" has here proved a disastrous criterion for prose style. The American architect Frank Lloyd Wright once drew a distinction much to our purpose. "Plainness," he said, "although simple, is not what I mean by simplicity.

Simplicity is a clean, direct expression of that essential quality of the thing which is the nature of the thing itself." The new *NEB* translation is plain; the King James Version attains simplicity. Clarity is simple, not plain.

If clarity indicates a successful relationship between reader and writer, pleasure makes part of the success. The Books caution us repeatedly to remember the audience. But the pleasure in good prose will presumably be there for writer as well as reader. A writer may write for her own pleasure, less from zeal to communicate than from love of words. Furthermore, style will influence *what* a writer "wants" to say. People want to say what they are good at saying, can say most gracefully. The Books imply a one-time-process psychology of authorship. The spirit moves me to speak. I search for words, put proper words in proper places, do justice to the concept beneath. But this simplistic model does violence to both human motives and the power of words. Simple communication as motive will prevail only when all men are good and all things well. Even if I pick up my pen pure in heart, words cajole me. If I succeed in saying what I think, I rejoice because the act of writing has, in a sense, told me, made me see, what I think. The old Oscar Wilde jibe, "How do I know what I think until I hear what I say?" is literally true. Even purely expository prose less describes a truth than reveals one. The Books warn that idea-in-mind must always precede pen-in-hand. And we must always revise. Don't the two contradict each other? Our idea is clarified in the writing. We then think again, the idea before us. Words form idea. Then the reverse. This becomes a process, not a one-time event. Ernst Cassirer cautions in *The Logic of the*

Humanities: "It is never simply a question of imparting information, but of statement and response. It is only in this twofold process that true thought emerges" (p. 113).

Another of The Books' dogmas is "Control words! Don't let them control you!" However, clarity as a process rather than a one-time relationship would seem to indicate a relationship between words and writer more complex than this. The writer controls words. Then they, as her first draft, control her. She then again, as revisor, controls them. *Da capo.* Clarity, thus, is an ever closer approximation of sentence to concept, involves a surrender to words as well as a victory over them. We can see here one of The Books' fundamental errors. They use a static, rather than a dynamic, model of verbal composition. It is not entirely true that ideas matter and words don't. It is not entirely true that you have not really had an idea until you've expressed it in words. Both are half-truths, stages of a process. In Western philosophy's long-standing quarrel between idealism and realism, The Books remain realists. Reality is "out there" and words must remain loyal to it.

A complete theory of prose style need not, indeed cannot, settle this endless dispute. But it should chart the whole dispute. It should account for a prose loyal to a preexistent reality, and it should account for a prose loyal to words themselves as a final reference point. For the act of composition, as we have just seen, employs both perspectives, oscillates from realism to idealism and back again. Clarity, as a prose ideal, alternates a faith in things with a faith in words. The Books omit half the process. They thus ground themselves on both a false theory of knowledge and a false theory of perception. They assume both a neutral observer whom psychology has long ago disproved and a neutral language that even science has now discarded. Custom distinguishes expository prose from creative or fictional. The language of fiction, as David Lodge has made clear in a book of this name, cannot be judged by its fidelity to a preexisting reality. It creates the things it describes and thus cannot be anything *but* faithful. Clarity in prose keeps faith to just such a created reality. If we make a spectrum with the King James's passage from Matthew at one end and a telegram ("Uncle George died Mon Stop Funeral Wed Stop Come") at the other, we can say the whole spectrum is clear, but that most prose will tend to fall toward the Matthew end, true less to circumstance than to the inner logic of its own form. It will always try, that is, to suffuse fidelity-to-concept with pleasure, to inform it with attitude.

The impulse to do this shows up everywhere. When a World War II aircraft pilot radios back to his ship "Sighted sub, sunk same," he has at heart a message about himself as well as about the submarine. He wants to tell us *in what spirit* he sank the submarine, how he felt about his accomplishment. Such laconic insouciance has been created by his style. Alliteration, like rhyming and pun, is fun in itself, taking us, as Freud points out, back to a childhood where words were senseless, pure oral pleasure. Here the pilot's joy in his accomplishment shines drolly through the childlike soundplay. He can afford the high spirits, the uncontrolled play because his deed implies a countervailing discipline.

We thus uncover an irony. The theory of prose as a *descriptive* medium, neutral, denotative, is willing to sacrifice pleasure for clarity. Might it be that clarity finally *depends* on pleasure? That it embraces artifice rather than abandoning it? Prose, this argument leads us to assert, can never be forced into neutral statement for long. It always resists this pressure, and rightly. It wants to escape back to the eloquence—the poetry —from which it came. In doing so, it flees not to excrescent ornament but to its natural home. We might invert the classical relationship between the two. A traditional theorist argues:

> All the qualities of good style may be ranged under two heads, perspicuity and ornament. For all that can possibly be required of language is, to convey our ideas clearly to the minds of others and, at the same time, in such a dress, as by pleasing and interesting them, shall most effectively strengthen the impressions which we seek to make. (Hugh Blair, Lecture 10 of *Lectures on Rhetoric and Belles Lettres*)

Instead, think of ornament, pure pleasure in pure form, as the center, and the ideas conveyed as clever enough to hitch a ride on the vehicle of delight.

Let us test these speculations about attitude on the norm itself, Dryden's prose. Here he begins the *Preface to the Fables, Ancient and Modern:*

> 'Tis with a poet, as with a man who designs to build, and is very exact, as he supposes, in casting up the cost beforehand; but, generally speaking, he is mistaken in his account, and reckons short of the expense he first intended. He alters his mind as the work proceeds, and will have this or that convenience more, of which he had not thought when he began. So has it happened to me; I have built a house, where I intended but a lodge; yet with better success than a nobleman, who, be-

ginning with a dog kennel, never lived to finish the palace he had contrived. (p. 387)

A well-known discussion of prose style lays it down "quite generally that the use of metaphor tends to obscure the essential nature of prose because it substitutes a poetic equivalence for a direct statement." Dryden begins with an extended simile between the poet and the man who builds, and then embraces the simile as a metaphor: "I have built a house, where I intended but a lodge." Further, he has built upon the relation of simile to metaphor the rhetorical *gradatio* (climax) that furnishes the structure for his opening paragraph. He opens with the initial comparison, then spells it out: casting the account, reckoning short, altering his mind, more conveniences. Then a transition, "So it has happened to me," prepares us for the climactic metaphor, "I have built a house, where I intended but a lodge." The opening structure ends with an illustrative anecdote, itself metaphorical, which invites us to ponder—and modify—the basic metaphor. The first section of the *Preface* aims to describe the genesis of the *Fables*. Dryden, starting humbly, built more largely than he intended, but did not, like the nobleman, start *meanly* upon a grandiose purpose. Nor, like him, has he failed to finish his design, enlarged though it be.

Dryden does not worry this opening metaphor to death but he does, in what follows, build on it. The house is given a family, the family of English poets, and these have their generations, of which Dryden is one. The metaphor stands as reference point and illustrative touchstone for what follows. Thus clarity in its real sense, a carefully orchestrated reader-writer relationship, here *begins* with metaphor, and in a fairly complex way. Dryden does not invite us to pause and ponder as I have done. But this does not mean he has not contrived his "clarity" carefully. You can see it in the syntax, which follows his thought, like the housemaker's purpose, as it proceeds in its unpremeditated turnings. "'Tis with . . . and . . . as he supposes . . . but . . . and . . . So has it . . . yet with . . ." The prose recreates, in a model, how Dryden's mind had moved in creating the book. The Books, of course, permit none of this metaphorical hanky-panky. They would rewrite it something like this: "I did not intend, at first, to write so long a book." Dryden's far more poetic clarity breaks all the rules for being clear.

Dryden remains, furthermore, wedded to this metaphorical strategy. Here is a later passage from the *Preface:*

> With this account of my present undertaking I conclude the first part of this discourse: in the second part, as at a second sitting, though I alter not the draught, I must touch the same features over again, and change the dead-colouring of the whole. (p. 390)

He thus summarizes the self-portraiture of himself as old and infirm that had immediately preceded this graceful transition, and also prepares for the defense of himself and his method of translation that follows. He wants the picture of himself as old, worn, yet vigorous to stay in his reader's eye. He chooses again, as in the opening paragraph, the illustrative anecdote, the picture:

> I leave them ["some original papers of my own"] wholly to the mercy of the reader. I will hope the best, that they will not be

condemned; but if they should, I have the excuse of an old gentleman, who, mounting on horseback before some ladies, when I was present, got up somewhat heavily, but desired of the fair spectators that they would count fourscore and eight before they judged him. By the mercy of God, I am already come within twenty years of his number, a cripple in my limbs, but what decays are in my mind, the reader must determine. (pp. 389–90)

How cleverly the anecdote puts us just where Dryden wants us. If we criticize his book, we are like a young lady laughing at a venerable octogenarian.

Dryden's prose in the *Preface* remains, in fact, metaphorical throughout. Not only does he repeatedly refer to the "thread of his discourse," but his "verses swell," Virgil warms him by degrees, Homer sets him on fire all at once, the English poets become a family with, as father, a Chaucer who was "a little dipt in the rebellion of the Commons." Anecdote and digression, proverb and quotation, easy conversational— almost associational—syntax, a reflectional restatement and self-questioning which casts the reader in his implied role in the *Preface*'s argument—all these build a contrived, artificial prose. Plain statement, meaning pure and semantic, "that absolute precision of statement which is the mark of excellent prose," supply but the beginning of Dryden's purpose. Such prose as he writes aims above all at *tone,* creating a certain reader-writer relationship. And this relationship remains drenched in qualities, emotions, attitudes. The clarity it attains is Frank Lloyd Wright's simplicity, form and purpose congruent. If Dryden is the model of English prose, then prose provides the vehicle of *attitude* as much as of statement or description. Dryden's prose works in this world not, as The Books recommend, in the next.

Afterthoughts

I'M NOT THE first person to suggest that decoration was a primary human need, an essence rather than an adornment. The Scottish essayist and historian Thomas Carlyle, for one, got there before me: "The first purpose of clothes . . . was not warmth or decency, but ornament; . . . the first spiritual want of a barbarous man is Decoration." We are deeply committed to thinking the opposite: *Obviously,* the first purpose of clothes was to keep warm. *Obviously,* their second purpose was to cover up our private parts. *Obviously,* ornament had to wait for Prada and Gucci. Likewise with prose style, its first purpose is to get the message across with no frills. Frills automatically make you suspicious. But what if ornament came first? Ornament is driven by pleasure, not by dos and don'ts and threats of time in the penalty box. That's the "What if?" I entertained in this chapter.

Is it really such a strange suggestion? Let us return for a moment to the yesteryear of composition instruction via that best of travelling companions, Sister Miriam Joseph. In *Shakespeare's Use of the Arts of Language,* the vade mecum that I mentioned in *Origins,* she "present[s] to the modern reader the general theory of composition current in Shakespeare's England" (p. 3). We may take it as the English version of the classical rhetorical curriculum, of the "way things used to be." Of the classical "trivium" come down to earth and actually taught. And of what the greatest verbal imagination that has ever lived made of this classical curriculum. It is a tough read, full of complex verbal and logical analysis. No self-cancelling general moral exhortations here. Rather, above all, a *descriptive vocabulary,* a nomenclature. The teaching proceeds through examples, hundreds of them. It is like a first-year biology class. Look and Describe. What are the lessons taught there?

Well, above all a complex nomenclature to describe how language works. A curriculum like this teaches you about language in the same way that the periodic table teaches you chemistry. How could this possibly be any fun? It is fun because when you know the names for things you take greater pleasure in them. A walk in the woods is a much deeper experience if you know the names of the trees. In a fundamental sense, you know where you are. And what happens then, as you walk through this woodland of words? Something the "clarity" clichés ignore. You begin to see this nomenclature as a catalogue of possible decoration. You see that you can look at language in a different way, look *at* it rather than *through* it. You can read as if our first need is decoration.

That is the deepest lesson that the study of classical rhetoric teaches us. It is certainly, and I mean certainly, the lesson that Shakespeare learned. Read his plays after an immersion in Sister Miriam's world and you see a language always in surplus. He is always saying things the hard way. He is always looking *at* the verbal surface, whether it is a figure of speech (he builds the whole of his narrative poem *Venus and Adonis* on one rhetorical figure, *chiasmus*) or, as in *Hamlet,* writing a play about the kind of play (revenge tragedy) which he is writing.

An ordinary example from Sister Miriam just for fun. Here is how Romeo says "It is dawn, my love."

> Look, love, what envious streaks
> Do lace the severing clouds in yonder East.
> Night's candles are burnt out, and jocund day
> Stands tiptoe on the misty mountain tops.
> (*Romeo and Juliet* 3.5.7–10)

Sister Miriam cites this passage (p. 129) to illustrate *chronographia,* description of the time. Such a terminology does not tell you much, you might say. Oh, but it does. It makes you ask, "Well, *how* does it tell us what time it is?" The whole scene takes on human life. The sky becomes "envious" of Romeo and Juliet's happiness in one another. The stars are domesticated into night's candles, and day becomes a jocund giant standing tiptoe on the misty mountains. Four lines animate the earth and sky. To assign a *name* to the passage is to insist that the reader look *at* it rather than *through* it. Aha! a new world, a new kind of reality, in reference to which the language is "clear."

Again, you might say, "But this is *poetry:* No fair!" It is my business in *Style: An Anti-Textbook* to argue that prose works the same way. You have to credit the new world it can create, just as you do here. And it is created through—if you insist that a passage like this just says, "It is dawn"—a particular kind of education in words, the rhetorical education which gave Shakespeare the means to be Shakespeare.

I quoted the architect Thomas Hastings's aphorism on style: "the job done." But what we need, after The Books' moral exhortations, is instruction on *how* the job is done.

Showing how the job is done was what the classical rhetorical curriculum was all about. Today, this curriculum has been almost completely lost, or rather discarded. It is too hard, too much like chemistry or physics, too full of incontrovertible assertions (a *chiasmus* really is a *chiasmus* 'til the end of time). And pleasure in words for their own sake has gone with it.

This is more than a great pity because the job to be done has become much more complex. The signals we broadcast are increasingly a package of words, sounds, and images, and each of these has its own kind of clarity. The Books' advice becomes even more self-contradictory and useless in such a mixture of oral and inscribed communication. The late philosopher of business Peter Drucker argued that the central task today is improving the productivity of knowledge workers, just as industrialization improved the productivity of manual workers. In this new task, which is a task of communication, I was, in the first edition of this book, and am still now, bold enough to join Shakespeare in urging that "No profit grows where is no pleasure taken." We are going to need the full range of human communication; we are going to need, that is, an education in *eloquence.* Have we made any progress toward this end since I wrote this chapter? I will state candidly and openly, as the diplomats say, that we could hardly be further away from seeing this need, understanding it, and putting it into practice than we are at present.

A few more words on a richer definition of "clarity." I've argued in this chapter that we ought to let the reality to which we are being clear and faithful vary, as well as the style that we use to describe it. Think about this for a minute. Isn't such an attitude the very mechanism of human tolerance? Instead of saying, "No, no, that's a terrible way to say it!" (and we very often do this and have to), might we also learn to say, "Well, suppose she's not an idiot, but just trying to describe a reality I can't see? What might that reality be like?" Describing new kinds of realities is what verbal eloquence is all about; it is what Sister Miriam's curriculum is all about. We see here the connection between eloquence and moral judgment. We need a richer understanding of the mechanisms of tolerance just as much as we need a richer understanding of human productivity, and eloquence—the pleasure in words for their own sake—stands at the center of both endeavors. As Carlyle urged us to see, and the classical education in words demonstrated, ornament can be essence.

I said some unkind things about college teaching. I would qualify that now. I was talking about university teaching, and research university teaching at that. And here, perhaps, there has been some improvement, though from what I can see, not much. Teaching in undergraduate colleges is as intense as it has always been, perhaps more so. That is why undergraduate colleges are such a bargain in the current market for brand-name university degrees.

Composition teaching at the college level has improved both in theory and in practice. The composition world has acknowledged that there are different kinds of prose for different academic specializations and professions. It is a step on the road to a course in prose style. But there are still few, very few, courses in prose style.

The unkind things I said about university administrative prose stand unqualified. It gets worse and worse. So, too, as far as I can see, does undergraduate writing. And the errors common in undergraduate papers now appear regularly in the daily newspapers. Subject-verb agreement ought not to be beyond the powers of people who write for a living (you need only know how to count to two), but it often is. And, to segue from grammar to eloquence, sentence shape seems often but a memory. Here is a two-sentence example, by no means the worst that could be chosen, from a recent *Wall Street Journal* column; the prose reads like the goop extruded from a frozen custard machine:

> GM Chief Rick Wagoner merely contented himself with venting to the L.A. Times a few weeks ago about his own leaking board, though the GM leaks were more manipulative than any that came from H-P. Coke's board, which then featured investing legend Warren Buffett, was a veritable leakfest two years ago during its hunt for a CEO, when one name after another surfaced in the press, including that of Gillette's James Kilts, who abruptly withdrew from consideration

A final update. In the first edition, I suggested that a university president's salary might be $50,000. Now university presidents are paid ten times as much to write the same kind of prose.

3 The Opaque Style

> My theory has always been that the public will accept style,
> provided you do not call it style either in words or by, as it were,
> standing off and admiring it.
>
> *Raymond Chandler Speaking*

PROSE STYLE KNOWS but a single taxonomy: the classification into high, middle, and low. That this has lasted with little protest from Cicero's day to our own demonstrates its flexibility more than its precision, but any explanation of the Expository Prose Vision Moralized must pass through it to a more satisfactory categorization. The threefold division emerges from an earlier one, earlier in logic as well as time: thought will demand one style, emotion another. Thought will find a style that is logical, clear, unornamental, largely unpatterned. Emotion will devise a different strategy, appealing through form and stock response rather than through clarity and logic. These set down two poles: teach thinking and move feeling. An intermediate position pops up like a mushroom. It will do something of both. Argue with feeling, move with logic.

These three positions form the basis for several discriminations. We discriminate by purposes: reason within the low style, move in the high, or "conciliate" (as Cicero calls it) by some combination. Or we separate by subject: high style for serious subject, low for humble tasks of ordering life, middle for the mixed world between or small subject that promises greatly. But neither purpose nor subject tells us about the style itself, the pattern of words. Three additional specific criteria can animate the threefold division: syntax, diction, density of ornament. The high style chooses specialized or unfamiliar or highly resonant words and puts them into careful patterns of balance, antithesis, and climax. It allows itself the ornaments of sound (alliteration, assonance, rhyme), puns, the whole range of metaphor and simile, the pleasures of repetition and restatement. The low style uses none of these; the middle style, some, but moderately and in moderate combination.

Such a tripartite scheme contains its paradoxes. At moments of great stress or significance, the flattest cliché, the most obviously "low" of low styles, can take on supreme dignity—so King Lear, when he meets the returned Cordelia:

> Pray, do not mock me:
> I am a very foolish fond old man,
> Fourscore and upward, not an hour more nor less;
> And, to deal plainly,
> I fear I am not in my perfect mind.
> (*King Lear* 4.7.59–63)

We can moralize the three stages. The high style, whatever its syntax, diction, or logical appeal, will be that style which "achieves a vision of society which draws speaker and hearers together into a closer bond." "It is," Northrop Frye continues in *The Well-Tempered Critic*, "the voice of the genuine individual reminding us of our genuine selves, and of our role as members of a society, in contrast to a mob" (p. 44). This style moves the audience, but it includes its antithesis, the style that teaches them. Frye unites the two purposes that classical antiquity had seen as disparate. He builds his transcendence on imagination, the unity of thought and feeling. This unity is the high style's effect on the audience. Effect thus finally defines style. The concomitant definition, which Frye goes on to describe, proceeds from the moral purpose of the speaker:

> High style in ordinary speech is heard whenever a speaker is honestly struggling to express what his society, as a society, is trying to be and do. It is even more unmistakably heard, as we should expect, in the voice of the individual facing a mob, or some incarnation of the mob spirit, in the death speech of Vanzetti, in Joseph Welch's annihilating rebuke of McCarthy during the McCarthy hearings, in the dignity with which a New Orleans mother explained her reasons for sending her white child to an unsegregated school. All these represent in different ways the authority of high style in action, moving, not on the middle level of thought, but on the higher level of imagination and social vision. (pp. 45–46)

It is such careful thinking and brilliant example as this which underlie the mechanical call for sincerity in books on prose style. Yet offered even so ably, such a definition presents problems. Sincerity wears many masks. Few of us speak all our minds all the time, thank Heaven. The "genuine self" of which Frye speaks is, literally, an act of faith. And how do we judge "the closer bond" produced by a genuine high style? "Such style has a peculiar quality of penetration about it: it elicits a shock of recognition, as it is called, which is the proof of its genuineness." What help is this? Just as the scientific criterion for prose, conceptual clarity, demands a preexisting concept to be clear about, so the moral criterion for prose implies a morality to be true to. No morality, no shock of recognition. Frye has little patience for the "high style = ornamental style" equation: "High style in this sense is emphatically not the high-flown style: all ornate language in rhetoric belongs to the middle style, the language of society engaged in routine verbal ritual" (pp. 44–45). The real criteria for the high style must be moral, not aesthetic.

The trouble with the tripartite division is not that it is vague and thus inapplicable. It is so vague it is nearly always applicable—especially so if you redefine it thoroughly, either morally or affectively. You can even adapt it to the dictates of clarity and scientific prose. The high style becomes bad, the middle good, and the low "colloquial." No, the trouble lurks in the tripartite division itself. Because it renders comparison invidious, it introduces the dispute that invidious comparison inevitably brings. It cannot just describe, it must evaluate. Which purposes are best? Which subjects most serious? Who, what, most moral? More than this, it has repeatedly proved itself tone-deaf. It can tell you what was said and explain why it was said that way, but it seldom reveals the *spirit* in which it was said. It defines badly the kind of agreement struck between writer and reader. It forces us, finally, to take an attitude toward style, whether the attitude be formal (diction, syntax, density of figures), moral (as with Frye's definition), or scientific. It asks us, in the composition course, to teach things that cannot be taught.

Since no other categorization has ever been offered, one must be devised. Instead of a hierarchical, vertical metaphor, picture a horizontal one—a spectrum. Instead of three "steps" or "styles," allow an infinite number. Instead of morality, effect on the audience, conceptual clarity, or ornament, try to measure a psychological variable, stylistic self-consciousness. To what degree does a writer acknowledge his style *as a style?* To what degree are we to *feel* the style as such? To what degree, that is, does the style realize itself as opaque, as—the enemy of clarity—a style to be looked *at* rather than *through?* Finally, what implications for prose style, and for the teaching of prose style, does such a categorization bring?

Here are three exemplary styles. The high-middle-low nomenclature yields results very different from the opaque style spectrum. First, a passage from Hemingway's *A Farewell to Arms:*

The waiter brought a dish of sauerkraut with a slice of ham over the top and a sausage buried in the hot wine-soaked cabbage. I ate it and drank the beer. I was very hungry. I watched the people at the table in the cafe. At one table they were playing cards. Two men at the table next me were talking and smoking. The cafe was full of smoke. The zinc bar, where I had breakfasted, had three people behind it now; the old man, a plump woman in a black dress who sat behind a counter and kept track of everything served to the tables, and a boy in an apron. I wondered how many children the woman had and what it had been like.

When I was through with the *choucroute* I went back to the hospital. The street was all clean now. There were no refuse cans out. The day was cloudy but the sun was trying to come through. I rode upstairs in the elevator, stepped out and went down the hall to Catherine's room, where I had left my white gown. I put it on and pinned it in back at the neck. I looked in the glass and saw myself looking like a fake doctor with a beard. I went down the hall to the delivery room. The door was closed and I knocked. No one answered so I turned the handle and went in. The doctor sat by Catherine. The nurse was doing something at the other end of the room.

"Here is your husband," the doctor said. (pp. 328–29)

By aesthetic criteria, this is surely the low style: no ornament, no wordplay, a commonplace choice of words, above all, syntactic simplicity, almost exclusively simple and compound sentences. Effect on the audience? Low style again. The novelist deliberately avoids playing on our feelings. Dignity of subject? Low style again, for the passage deals with ordinary experience. The morality criterion seems impossible to apply here.

Now a passage in the middle style, a selection from Somerset Maugham's essayistic intellectual autobiography, *The Summing Up:*

For to write good prose is an affair of good manners. It is, unlike verse, a civil art. Poetry is baroque. Baroque is tragic, massive and mystical. It is elemental. It demands depth and insight. I cannot but feel that the prose writers of the baroque period, the authors of King James's Bible, Sir Thomas Browne, Glanville, were poets who had lost their way. Prose is a rococo art. It needs taste rather than power, decorum rather than inspiration and vigour rather than grandeur. Form for the poet is the bit and the bridle without which (unless you are an acrobat) you cannot ride your horse; but for the writer of prose it is the chassis without which your car does not exist. It is not an accident that the best prose was written when rococo, with its elegance and moderation, at its birth attained its greatest excellence. For rococo was evolved when baroque had become declamatory and the world, tired of the stupendous, asked for restraint. It was the natural expression of persons who valued a civilized life. Humour, tolerance and horse sense made the great tragic issues that had preoccupied the first half of the seventeenth century seem excessive. The world was a more comfortable place to live in and perhaps for the first time in centuries the cultivated classes could sit back and enjoy their leisure. It has been said that good prose should resemble the conversation of a well-bred man. Conversation is only possible when men's minds are free from pressing anxieties. Their lives must be reasonably secure and they must have no grave concern about their souls. They must attach importance to the refinements of civilization. They must value courtesy, they must pay attention to their persons (and have we not also been told that good prose should be like the clothes of a well-dressed man, appropriate but unobtrusive?), they must fear to bore, they must be neither flippant nor solemn, but always apt; and they must look upon "enthusiasm" with a critical glance. This is a soil very suitable for prose. (pp. 38–39)

A style calculated to convey information, this. The civilized style of the English essay that Maugham is talking about, he also illustrates. His prose embodies the middle style par excellence. It does not offer the calculated simplicity of diction and syntax that Hemingway chose, yet it doesn't fetch words from afar either. Nobody would think the syntax contrived. An important subject is described but not a great one. It both discusses good manners and displays them in its open, easy, yet not informal address to the reader, one appropriate but unobtrusive.

Now here is a third passage, from James Gould Cozzens's novel *By Love Possessed:*

Accepting the filled sherry glass, Julius Penrose took a swallow. "This unhappy event has several unhappy aspects," he said. "Well, we owe nature a death, I'm told. By our choosing to be born, we contracted for death. Recision would be inequitable and unjust. Let me hear no more complaining! The terms of payment? Not exorbitant, I think. What could be more generous? If we pay this year, we won't have to pay next year." He took another sip of sherry. "Regarding the dead, our pious rule is nothing if not good. Ralph, let us agree, is a little bastard; and you won't suppose I mean by the term that Alice Detweiler could have ever had the appetite, let alone the imagination, to play George false. Helen is known to have been faithful and true, good and self-sacrificing, and, perhaps not so relevant, but they are qualities in the main admired, chaste and pure. She is, therefore, virtue; Ralph is vice. Because of all this virtue, Helen's sorrows, her sufferings, the last full measure of her rash act, put her publicly, in terms of public opinion, unassailably in the right. Everybody must feel that."

Julius Penrose took a sip of sherry. "Yes; I too feel it; but do I think it? An entrance is won to the heart: but to the head? Passion and reason, self-division's cause! I'm afraid I think that this gentle and unspotted soul was and is, has been and now always will be, very much in the wrong. On people as people, I try never to pass judgment—we can seldom know what the real truth about them is. Yet on acts, acts of theirs, I see no reason to hesitate in passing judgment—this is good; this is bad; this is mean; this is kind. On such points, I'm competent, as every man is. Like the common law, we secular moralists aren't interested in the why; we observe the what. Here, the what that gives me pause is this. Ralph's a little bastard; yes. Something ought to have been done to and about him, I'd think preferably with a horsewhip, if nowadays one could be found. Be good, or I'll beat you! That's in order. That's fair warning and fair play. Could the same be said of a verbal threat to do a thing like this—Ralph must be good, or Helen will kill herself? And how much less, if, for mere threat, performance is substituted? No; there is a want of principle, which is to say, too much feeling. I pronounce this bad. I pronounce this mean. The sentence, of course, is on the act, not the person. I pity the person; I take her to be mad, possessed by love. Her feelings acted. Here is simply more of feeling's comic or tragic, yet, to the feeler, always juicy, fruits. I quote: 'A warmth within the breast would melt the freezing reason's colder part. And like a man in wrath, the heart stood up and answered: I have felt!' Let us pass on. Your refection is spread; take some." (pp. 546–47)

Within the traditional categories, the style is high. The subject is serious, the occasion climactic. The reader's feelings are carefully enlisted by a series of verbal artifices. A special legal diction, for example, icy and remote (recision, inequitable, pass judgment, competent, in order, the sentence, I pronounce) contrasts with the situation's macabre immediacy, a Helen who has drunk half a bottle of cleaning fluid. Cozzens plans his sentences to have—and show—the balance, antithesis, parenthesis, and climax usually called "periodic":

Helen is known to have been faithful and true,
                                good and self sacrificing
and (perhaps not so relevant, but
they are qualities ((in the main)) admired)
                                chaste and pure.
She is (therefore)   virtue;
Ralph is   vice.

Cozzens develops a situation already resonant with literary symbolism, a "refection," a ceremonial communion meal, and spices it with quotations, "Passion and reason, self-division's cause"; buried quotations, "the last full measure of her rash act"; echoes of the Book of Common Prayer, "was and is, has been and now always will be"; proverbial allusion, "our pious rule" (*de mortuis nihil nisi bonum;* of the dead speak nothing if not good); and popular allusion, the "juicy fruits" of Juicy Fruit chewing gum. He allows himself the kind of repetitive elaboration, the savoring of a word by redefinition, that older English prose was fond of: "publicly, in terms of public opinion," "unhappy event . . . unhappy aspects." Julius Penrose is given to that kind of reasoning-with-oneself-aloud ("Let me hear no more complaining! The terms of payment? Not exorbitant, I think. What could be more generous?") which classical rhetoricians called *hypophora*. We might even fit the passage into Frye's exclusive definition of the high style, in spite of the verbal artifice. For Julius Penrose is very valiantly trying to express what he and Arthur Winner, and the society they constitute, really feel about the suicide, how sense is to be made of it.

We have, then, reasonable samples of the three styles as traditionally defined. (Two of the three are prose fiction; this raises problems to be considered later.) The process of categorizing tells us something about them but, distorting a good deal, ignores more. Placing them on a self-consciousness spectrum renders the invidious high-middle-low order oddly undescriptive. Posit the two extremes of our spectrum. Both are unliterary. At the extreme left, childish babble, nursery rhymes, pure pleasure in words. Words here are things. You play with them. They have shape, sound, corporeality. At the other end, a mathematical equation, pure significance, all sign. Pleasure flows from concepts. Nonsense rhyme presents a perfectly opaque surface, equations a perfectly transparent one. Between two such extremes all prose should embody a continuous spectrum. Scientific prose falls far toward the right, equation side; here Dryden and Swift, so mistakenly considered monuments to clarity, are glued down. Correspondingly, on the left we find the prose of *Finnegan's Wake;* a little further to the right, *Ulysses;* further, *Dubliners.* Maugham's prose, as in our example, lives and moves in the middle. But both Hemingway and Cozzens would occupy the same position, to the left of Maugham. In both, style is to be seen as such, symbolic opacity.

By fleeing the high style, Hemingway dramatizes a flight from everything it represents. His syntax stops with too studied a simplicity. It cautions us, by its very divergence from normative prose, to notice it as a syntax. So, too, does the style as a whole—diction, rhythm, tone—a low style that wants to be seen as a low style. Style stands in deliberate contrast to situation. Fredric Henry, under great pressure, endures the climax of his love for Catherine Barkley just as we endure the climax of the novel. Hemingway intensifies the low style at this point. Why? To symbolize the hero's attitude toward the pressure. The style—deliberate, maximally controlled, utterly plain—symbolizes, indeed creates the heroism. The act of stylistic control stands for the controlled feelings the hero (and such control *is* his heroism) cannot express directly. Hemingway thus plays against the old tripartite stylistic expectancy. We expect a speech on stoic endurance of grief. He offers the opposite, a new kind of bravery.

We can see this only if we acknowledge the style as such, look *at it* and not *through it.* The opaque segment of the spectrum, by compelling this attention to surface, guides with more accuracy to the passage's center. Only attention to the stylistic surface yields the meaning it adumbrates—a meaning not beneath it but on it. By the canons of conceptual clarity, such a reflective surface stands triple-damned. In the words of James Sutherland:

> Style, of course, is not just a patina that gathers on the surface of old prose; but when we become too conscious of style it is either because the writer himself was too conscious of it while he was writing, or because his prose is already moribund and is beginning to give off the characteristic aroma of antiquity. (*On English Prose*, p. 28)

It should be clear by now how such a conception misleads. A writer cannot be, for a certain range of effects, too conscious of style or make us too conscious of it. Yet Cozzens has been called names for doing just this, just what has earned Hemingway his title of plain stylist. In the Cozzens passage, as with *A Farewell to Arms,* context reveals how the style works. Julius Penrose ends his homily with "Your refection is spread; take some." Here is what immediately follows:

> "I'm not hungry," Arthur Winner said. "Julius, how long have you known that Noah's accounts were short?"
>
> "Ah!" Julius Penrose said. "Well, I'm not sorry to have you ask! Yes: that's where I was putting off getting."

The whole "refection" speech, so carefully bounded by sherry at the beginning and biscuit at the end, functions as a digressive evasion of the hard business to be talked. The nice blend of periodic syntax and colloquiality that characterizes Julius Penrose is here only slightly exaggerated, but enough, with the concluding mention of "putting off," to tell us that he was making a speech and knew he was making a speech. The high style, indeed, fits the subject of the speech, but it becomes, given the fictional context, more than slightly ironical. Again, unless we can see the style as style, we shall go wide of its real function in the novel. Cozzens depends upon the three-style convention to illuminate his departure from it. His ironical, opaque high style needs a set of categories beyond high-middle-low, in other words, needs our spectrum.

The self-consciousness spectrum forces no preconceived attitudes upon us. Right is no higher than left. We need not judge the dignity of the subject, its decorum, its morality. Only a stylistic judgment is required. How should we attend to or "take" the style? Does it diminish into insignificance on the right or does it move left, growing so large in our consciousness as to become the subject? This is a fundamental question to ask about style, and the only one that does not force attitudinizing of one sort or another. It is possible, of course, to foist an attitude on the spectrum, most commonly the normative theorist's dislike of ornament. To this vagary, and to the spectrum's confutation of it, we must now turn.

The road of excess may lead to the palace of wisdom, as Blake asseverated, but for prose few have thought so. Stylistic excess has been suspect and scorned since Aristotle, whose *Rhetoric* cautions against letting style and persuasion show. The intended victims are put on guard, start patting their pockets. So, too, a style that seems oversize or unnecessary to the meaning is condemned. A famous critic asserts: "Style occurs in isolation only when it is bad, when it fails to coincide with meaning" (W. K. Wimsatt, *The Prose Style of Sam-*

uel Johnson, p. 10). This style for the sake of style Americans usually call "rhetoric," or verbal pyrotechnics. Opposite to rhetoric, the perfect union of thought and word falls well to the right in the spectrum; for only by detaching style from meaning can we see it as a self-conscious style:

> Rhetoric is the opposite of the process which I have called crystalization. Instead of condensing your emotion upon the cause, which becomes the symbol; instead of defining and making concrete your thought, by the aid of your sensuous perception; you give way to a mere verbal exaggeration of your feeling or your thought. (J. Middleton Murry, *The Problem of Style,* p. 118)

Such a distinction depends on the scientific attitude toward prose: all prose cherishes an object outside itself, a concept it must embody. When the language starts to cloud, it goes bad. But on the opaque-style spectrum, which does not render attitudinizing verdicts, it does not. It simply shifts its loyalty elsewhere, shifts it increasingly to the words themselves. Style *becomes* subject. You cannot then insist it ought to serve its subject. This, precisely, it does. Let us confront as an example, what has long been recognized as the most extreme stylistic extravagance, the most outrageous literary rhetoric in English, John Lyly's 1574 *Euphues, The Anatomy of Wit.* Here is a sample, long enough so you can get the feel of it. Euphues and his friend Philautus are slugging it out in an ordinary Euphuistic chat:

> Euphues had continual access to the place of Philautus and no little familiarity with him; and finding him at convenient leisure, in these short terms unfolded his mind unto him:

"Gentleman and friend, the trial I have had of thy manners cutteth off divers terms which to another I would have used in the like matter. And since a long discourse argueth folly, and delicate words incur the suspicion of flattery, I am determined to use neither of them, knowing either of them to breed offense. Weighing with myself the force of friendship by the effects, I studied ever since my first coming to Naples to enter league with such a one as might direct my steps, being a stranger, and resemble my manners, being a scholar; the which two qualities as I find in you able to satisfy my desire, so I hope I shall find a heart in you willing to accomplish my request. Which if I may obtain, assure yourself that Damon to his Pythias, Pylades to his Orestes, Titus to his Gysippus, Theseus to his Pirithous, Scipio to his Laelius, was never found more faithful than Euphues will be to Philautus."

Philautus by how much the less he looked for this discourse, by so much the more he liked it, for he saw all qualities both of body and mind in Euphues; unto whom he replied as followeth:

"Friend Euphues—for so your talk warranteth me to term you—I dare neither use a long process, neither a loving speech, lest unwittingly I should cause you to convince me of those things which you have already condemned. And verily I am bold to presume upon your courtesy, since you yourself have used so little curiosity, persuading myself that my short answer will work as great an effect in you as your few words did in me. And seeing that we resemble, as you say, each other in qualities, it cannot be that the one should differ from the other in courtesy. Seeing the sincere affection of the mind cannot be expressed by the mouth and that no art can unfold the entire love of the heart, I am earnestly to beseech you not to measure the firmness of my faith by the fewness of my words, but rather think that the overflowing waves of good will leave no passage for many words. Trial shall prove trust. Here is my hand, my heart, my lands, and my life at thy commandment. Thou mayest well perceive that I did believe thee that so soon I did love thee, and I hope thou wilt the rather love me in that I did believe thee."

Either Euphues and Philautus stood in need of friendship or were ordained to be friends. Upon so short warning to make so soon a conclusion might seem, in mine opinion, if it continued, miraculous; if shaken off, ridiculous. (pp. 141–42)

This is a typical passage. Others intensify these ornamental tricks. It is easy to see why scholars condemn the work with a puzzlement akin to religious wonder. But we might describe before we deplore. Antithetical balance and parallelism of all sorts scream the loudest:

direct my steps, being a stranger
resemble my manners, being a scholar
neither a long process—neither a long speech
firmness of my faith—fewness of my words
so short a warning—so soon a conclusion

Alliteration and assonance (beginning word rhyme) point to themselves repeatedly, especially in words occupying similar places in balanced or parallel constructions: folly / flattery; force of / friendship; looked for / liked it; long process / loving speech; firmness of / my faith; so short / as soon; my hand / my heart; my lands / and my life. And sometimes words that sound alike are put in similar places to draw them into antithesis:

And verily I am bold to presume upon your *courtesy*
since you yourself have used so little *curiosity*

Lyly dotes on proverbs ("Trial shall prove trust"), though not so much in this passage as elsewhere. He likes to build a climax:

1. Here is my hand
2. my heart
3. my lands
4. and my life
5. at thy commandment.

Notice here how the alliterative patterns of hand / heart and lands / life intersect the climactic structure and change the hand, lands, heart, life order which would supply the more usual scale of values. Similar endings often draw two words into antithesis: if it continued, miraculous; if shaken off, ridiculous. Occasionally Lyly will suspend the sense over a long, involved syntax that seems almost syllogistic:

> Seeing the sincere affection of the mind cannot be expressed by the mouth and that no art can unfold the entire love of the heart
> > I am earnestly to beseech you
> > > not to measure the firmness of my faith by the fewness of my words

The repetitions of single words and sometimes of phrases need no emphasis.

How to appraise such a style? The older classification calls it a high style, but a bad one, written by a stylistic compulsive. This has remained the common view. But in terms of a stylistic spectrum that does not force its attitudes on the reader, how does such a style work? It makes us acknowledge, as a first step, that Lyly wanted to interpose a vivid stylistic self-consciousness between himself and his readers—full left. Such self-conscious excess indicates an equally self-conscious bid for attention. Verbal ornament, as every lover of Shakespeare knows, enchanted the Elizabethans of Lyly's time. Lyly's bid for attention will be a virtuoso art. How far can a fairly limited grab bag of rhetorical tricks be carried? He will show them. *Euphues* did. It constituted, for Lyly, an elaborate bid for employment. He had no future. He wanted to become Revels Master. The job needed a witty, clever man. He would show how clever he was.

A style is a response to a situation. When you call a style bad, or exaggerated, much less mad, you ought to make sure you understand the situation it responds to. You may be objecting to the situation, not to the style invented to cope with it. So here. We object to the love of ornament, of words for their own sake, which engendered such extravagant verbal frivolity. And we object to a rhetorical showpiece consciously used as "advertisement for myself." We object to its exhibitionism. We wish prose to assume other, more familiar attitudes.

We might carry reflections on Euphuism and stylistic excess a step further by examining a letter of Flaubert's (quoted in Kenneth Burke's *Counter-Statement,* p. 6), who inherited quite another climate of prose attitudes, but still saw clearly what Lyly only half-knew he was after:

> What seems beautiful to me, what I should most like to do, would be a book about nothing, a book without any exterior ties, but sustained by the internal force of its style . . . a book which would have almost no subject, or at least in which the

subject would be almost invisible, if that is possible. The most beautiful works are those with the least matter.

Euphues goes on too long to be only a display-piece (in the old sense of the word, a "masterpiece"). It has a plot, but hardly one that matters—a prodigal-son moral a thousand times dead. Its characterization amounts to even less. It stands as the first document of English prose to view prose style with any attitude but the conceptual. Lyly is often damned as intoxicated. Well he might have been. He was the first to see new directions for prose and a new kind of relationship to his reader. He began to see that the logical development of prose would be from the conceptual or scientific attitude to the aesthetic or playful, from right spectrum to left.

His discovery came at the wrong time. England had just finished such a cycle in verse, and a reaction was about to set in. It brought with it the prose of Dryden and Swift, and the scientific attitude toward prose. We have had to complete an entire cycle to return to an attitude toward prose similar to Lyly's. It appears all over the fictional landscape these days in America, but most cleverly in Vladimir Nabokov's novel *Ada*. *Ada* is *Euphues* redivivus. Again, a selection long enough to give you the feel of the prose:

> How did the scuffle start? Did all three cross the brook stepping on slimy stones? Did Percy push Greg? Did Van jog Percy? Was there something—a stick? Twisted out of a fist? A wrist gripped and freed?
>
> "Oho," said Percy, "you are playful, my lad!"
>
> Greg, one bag of his plus-fours soaked, watched them helplessly—he was fond of both—as they grappled on the brink of the brook.

Percy was three years older, and a score of kilograms heavier than Van, but the latter had handled even burlier brutes with ease. Almost at once the Count's bursting face was trapped in the crook of Van's arm. The grunting Count toured the turf in a hunched-up stagger. He freed one scarlet ear, was retrapped, was tripped and collapsed under Van, who instantly put him "on his omoplates," *na lopatki,* as King Wing used to say in his carpet jargon. Percy lay panting like a dying gladiator, both shoulder blades pressed to the ground by his tormentor, whose thumbs now started to manipulate horribly that heaving thorax. Percy with a sudden bellow of pain intimated he had had enough. Van requested a more articulate expression of surrender, and got it. Greg, fearing Van had not caught the muttered plea for mercy, repeated it in the third person interpretive. Van released the unfortunate Count, whereupon he sat up, spitting, palpating his throat, rearranging the rumpled shirt around his husky torso and asking Greg in a husky voice to find a missing cufflink.

Van washed his hands in a lower shelf-pool of the brook and recognized, with amused embarrassment, the transparent tubular thing, not unlike a sea-squirt, that had got caught in the downstream course in a fringe of forget-me-nots, good name, too.

He had started to walk back to the picnic glade when a mountain fell upon him from behind. With one violent heave he swung his attacker over his head. Percy crashed and lay supine for a moment or two. Van, his crab claws on the ready, contemplated him, hoping for a pretext to inflict a certain special device of exotic torture that he had not yet had the opportunity to use in a real fight.

"You've broken my shoulder," grumbled Percy, half-rising and rubbing his thick arm. "A little more self-control, young devil."

"Stand up!" said Van. "Come on, stand up! Would you like more of the same or shall we join the ladies? The ladies? All right. But, if you please, walk in front of me now."

As he and his captive drew near the glade Van cursed himself for feeling rattled by that unexpected additional round; he was secretly out of breath, his every nerve twanged, he caught himself limping and correcting the limp—while Percy de Prey, in his magically immaculate white trousers and casually ruffled shirt, marched, buoyantly exercising his arms and shoulders, and seemed quite serene and in fact rather cheerful.

Presently Greg overtook them, bringing the cufflink—a little triumph of meticulous detection; and with a trite "Attaboy!" Percy closed his silk cuff, thus completing his insolent restoration.

Their dutiful companion, still running, got first to the site of the finished feast; he saw Ada, facing him with two stipple-stemmed red boletes in one hand and three in the other; and, mistaking her look of surprise at the sound of his thudding hooves for one of concern, good Sir Greg hastened to cry out from afar: "He's all right! He's all right, Miss Veen"—blind compassion preventing the young knight from realizing that she could not possibly have known yet what a clash had occurred between the beau and the beast.

"Indeed I am," said the former, taking from her a couple of her toadstools, the girl's favorite delicacy, and stroking their smooth caps. "And why shouldn't I be? Your cousin has treated Greg and your humble servant to a most bracing exhibition of Oriental Skrotomoff or whatever the name may be." (pp. 211–13)

Scuffle, start, stepping, slimy stones, something, stick, twisted, fist, wrist? Here are the old figures of sound again, the "brink of the brook" and "burlier brutes," which brought the scorn of centuries down on Lyly. Here is the same self-conscious agreement to look at, admire, join in the game of, the verbal surface. The "third person interpretive" and *na lopatki* replace Lyly's classical allusions and proverbial citations, but the purpose stays the same—to intensify our awareness of style. Nabokov has always been a virtuoso but never more than here. The calculated artifice of the dialogue, the strange diction ("meticulous detection," "insolent restoration," "dutiful companion"), with its slight parodistic echo of the chivalric "beau and the beast" archetype behind the passage, all invite not the breathless "Let me see life" attitude that scientific prose or realist fiction requires, but quite another. It says, rather, "How contrived, how literary, when it comes to that, most of our behavior is." The scientific stylist pictures a world where life as concepts comes first. The opaque stylist views experience differently: to him, life seems as stylized as literature. Ordinary experience seems fundamentally dramatic, a game of roles in which the self is not so much felt and possessed as presented and reenacted. For such an experience, the most faithful reflection will be a prose style equally contrived, literary, and self-conscious.

No one has, to my knowledge, criticized Nabokov for ornamental excess. This immunity may partly be explained by Nabokov's superior talent, or by the history of fiction separating him from Lyly. But it may also be because we now conceive of society, and of the self, in far more dramatic, literary terms than before. We perceive with less moral indignation the essential realism of the opaque style. The process that Lyly and Nabokov illustrate occurs pretty frequently, after all. "The artist's means," Kenneth Burke tells us, "are always tending to become ends in themselves" (*Counter-Statement,* pp. 54–55). When such a tendency coincides, as now, with widespread, systematic doubt of the veracity of language itself, pressure for an opaque style intensifies. A writer who has given up on words as "meaningful" will use them as stage prop, as scene, as theater decoration, symbolic action, absurdist gesture.

Not an exclusively literary temptation, this. It holds for American advertising as well as for Lyly or his fellow Elizabethan, Thomas Nashe. The scientific attitude toward Lyly's prose aside, look whither his absurdist syntactic gestures tend. *Euphues,* from its prodigal-son theme to its compulsive antithesis, constitutes a plea for balance. Its "excessive" ornament embodies an eloquent cry for the balanced view of experience and self which Lyly could not sustain in his own life. Viewed as such, Lyly's ornament works as essentially in his fiction as Nabokov's does in his, though in a different way. For both, structural pattern indicates tone, the reference pattern of articulation that tells writer and reader how they stand. The prejudice against ornament invoked by the scientific attitude should not govern other attitudes. Attack ornament and you attack the imagination itself: "Any speculation regarding ornament is a speculation upon the great power of the abstract and upon the infinite resources of the imaginary" (Henri Focillon, *The Life of Forms in Art,* p. 19).

From one point of view, then, there is no such thing as excessive ornament in prose. We can never be, as the hero of an Elizabethan romance complains, poisoned with roses, unless the poisoning constitutes the main business at hand. The denser the ornament, the more manner becomes matter, style subject, words things. Within such an aesthetic, Swift's cozy "proper words in proper places" becomes meaningless. All words are proper words, and proper places are the places the opaque stylist carves out as proper. The cloying sense of Walter Pater's fulsome writing must not cloud a fundamental attitude toward prose. "Mannerism"—manner become subject —constitutes as legitimate an attitude as any other. To it the sober pieties of Swift, Arnold ("The needful qualities for a fit prose," he insists in "The Study of Poetry," "are regularity, uniformity, precision, balance"), and The Books simply do not apply. (The argument here could be amplified, of course. Swift's "proper words" formula constitutes an absurdly inadequate description of his own prose and Arnold's "needful qualities" hardly begin to describe Arnoldian prose.)

Up to now, I've not discriminated between fictional and nonfictional prose. One might think the discrimination crucial. As David Lodge has pointed out, fictional prose roams freer than exposition because it points to no preexisting reality but creates one instead. Take this thought a step further. The fiction / nonfiction distinction is really one of differences in attitude toward prose. Fiction can exploit the scientific attitude as well as exposition. The line of fiction descending from Defoe uses expository prose. What difference does it make to prose stylists that Moll Flanders never lived? Diarists who have lived inhabit the same stylistic universe. Everything depends upon the prose attitude. As we can see by remembering the syllogistic Lyly passage, even the form of a syllogism embodies an aesthetic appeal, can be seen as opaque style, provided we are prepared to invoke that attitude and not the scientific one. Go a step further. Not only does the fiction / nonfiction distinction prove false for prose style, but the literary / nonliterary one as well. The range of stylistics, under the spectrum outlined, includes all verbal expression. Discriminate between literary and nonliterary and you have invoked the scientific attitude, admittedly or not. So René Wellek writes:

> Style may include all devices of speech that convey the attitude of the speaker (all "expressive language") and all devices that aim to achieve rhetorical ends, all devices for securing emphasis or explicitness, metaphor, rhetorical figures, syntactical patterns. Clearly, style embraces all speech and all writing. But stylistics as part of a science of literature must be concerned with much more special problems. (*Style in Language,* ed. T. A. Sebeok, p. 417)

The scientific prejudice inheres in such an assertion, even in trying to expel it. It seems clearer to distinguish two attitudes toward style, scientific and opaque, than to separate by conceptual referent into fictional and nonfictional.

The same confusion is often encountered when distinguishing poetry (or poetic prose) from prose (or "real" prose, Dryden's prose). So Morton Bloomfield, in an essay impressively titled "The Syncategorematic in Poetry":

> Poetic language calls attention to itself. . . . Poetic devices are the artist's weapons in his fight against the transitivity of lexical words [transitivity = outward references, words as "transparent"]. . . . When words lead to other words we are more conscious of their own wordhood than when they lead to concepts. (*Essays and Explorations,* p. 267)

Here is the same confusion of attitudes. Nothing but confusion has ever come from the effort to fix the poetry-prose boundary. It seems easier to isolate a scientific attitude toward prose that is also useful for some kinds of poetry. The opaque attitude proves useful for both. The stylistic spectrum, covering the whole range of expressivity from scientific to opaque, supplies an easier, more precise taxonomy than either fiction / exposition or prose / poetry. To say this only glosses Stendhal's definition of style: "Le style, c'est ajouter à une pensée donnée toutes les circonstances propres à produire tout l'effet que doit produire cette pensée" [Style adds to a thought all the circumstances needed to produce the whole effect which that thought ought to produce]. Are we to commit ourselves to thought with the feeling-tones that surround it or without them? Doing without them, we move toward the right end of the spectrum; with them, we move toward the left, toward Stendhal's, and our, opaque style.

Some pedagogical implications emerge from this theorizing. The teaching of composition in America has been overpoweringly scientific and normative. But if we seek stylistic self-consciousness—and I see no other goal for a writing course in America now—not so much normative measurement as range of comparative exercises seems called for. The pattern of expectation created by continual normative measurement continually confuses, for it does not apply to anything students read, only to what they write. They read the great stylists, or pieces of them, and are told to imitate. But these worthies range all over the stylistic spectrum, from the chilly transparency of *In Cold Blood* to the venerable opacities of

Sir Thomas Browne's "Urn-Burial." A normative, scientific attitude makes no sense for such a range of prose. Students, even slow ones, are not slow to see this. If both attitudes are to be taught, they ought to be made clear.

Instead, all the difficulties of the classical threefold scheme are introduced. A far more sensible procedure would dictate stylistic imitations such as an Elizabethan schoolboy did with his Virgil—imitate, compare student version and original, imitate again, compare once more—or the translation of one style into another. To hear the *sound* of prose, a student must be schooled on the figures of sound. To see the *shape* of prose, she needs the figures of arrangement. If she then wants to put all these resources, all these delights, behind her and write prose as sparklingly clear as Baccarat crystal, let her. But a student encouraged to write *only* neutral scientific prose will *never write it at all.* White light is made of colors. It cannot be constituted out of nothing. Neither can a student's knowledge of scientific prose. The route to scientific clarity, the clarity The Books urge upon us with elephantine humorlessness, lies through the charming meadows of ornament. No other path leads to the stylistic awareness where good prose begins.

We may come, joy of man's desiring, into a period of eloquence that demands the scientific attitude as a corrective. But we are not there yet. The rhetorical corrective is what we need now. Only it can teach that love of words for their own sake on which a healthy and joyful American prose can be built, taught, and learned. Only by seeing words, seeing prose style as a pleasure, can we have any idea of how it might, or why it should, be a duty.

Afterthoughts

I PONDERED OMITTING the *Euphues* example as being too remote for present tastes but decided to leave it in for just this reason. Provided that the reading is done self-consciously, the history of English prose teaches lessons that can be taught in no other way. This is as true of *Euphues* as it is of *Ada.* Apprentice writers need to sample work from all the periods of English prose just as a beginning pianist learns to play all the keys on the piano. In his memoir *A Mingled Chime,* Sir Thomas Beecham describes the system of self-study he invented when he was training himself to conduct. His teacher didn't know what to do with someone of his precocious talent, so Beecham invented a curriculum for himself:

> I used to select, or myself write, a shortish piece of two or three hundred bars and orchestrate it in the different styles of, say, Haydn, Bizet, Tschaikowsky or himself [his teacher], and very soon, I think, he extracted as much amusement from this pleasant game as I derived instruction. . . . I learned much from it that later on I was able to put to useful purposes. (p. 82)

I developed the stylistic spectrum argument further in later books: *Analyzing Prose* (2nd ed., 2003), *The Electronic Word* (1993), and *The Economics of Attention* (2006).

It may be that our first spiritual hunger is for Decoration, as Carlyle argues, but another hunger rivals it: the need for its absence, for plain speaking and plain dealing, for, as Shakespeare says, "Russet yeas and honest kersey noes." But the arguments for this plain style often run into the same self-contradictions that plague discussions of the opaque style. To take one example, E. B. Sledge wrote one of the great memoirs of World War II. In it, he tells what it was like to serve in the First Marine Division during the invasion of Peleliu and Okinawa. In his introduction to Sledge's chronicle, Paul Fussell writes:

> One cause of this book's distinction is that its author is not an "author." Sledge wrote this memoir less for strangers than to tell his own family what his war had been like. . . . The book is devoid of the literary expediencies and suavities that may occasion skepticism or disgust in more artistically self-conscious war memoirs. Sledge is so little an author in the pejorative sense that his eye seems never to wander from his subject to contemplate the literary effect he's creating. His style is like windowglass: you don't pause to notice it—you look through it to the actuality it discloses. It is this honesty, simplicity, and modesty that give Sledge's book its extraordinary power. (*With the Old Breed at Peleliu and Okinawa*, p. xi)

The problem is, Sledge's prose does not support what Fussell says: Sledge illustrates the paradox of at/through rather than explaining it. Here's a sample passage:

> The struggle for survival went on day after weary day, night after terrifying night. One remembers vividly the landings and the beachheads and the details of the first two or three days and nights of a campaign; after that, time lost all meaning. A lull of hours or days seemed but a fleeting instant of heaven-sent tranquility. Lying in a foxhole sweating out an enemy artillery or mortar barrage or waiting to dash across open ground under machine-gun or artillery fire defied any concept of time.
>
> To the noncombatants and those on the periphery of action, the war meant only boredom or occasional excitement; but to those who entered the meat grinder itself, the war was another

world of horror from which escape seemed less and less likely as casualties mounted and the fighting dragged on and on. Time had no meaning; life had no meaning. The fierce struggle for survival in the abyss of Peleliu eroded the veneer of civilization and made savages of us all. We existed in an environment totally incomprehensible to men behind the lines— service troops and civilians. (pp. 120–21)

Sledge confesses that he has spent time revising his prose from the rough notes he made at the time, and it shows. Parallel phrases: "day after weary day, night after terrifying night"; "Time had no meaning; life had no meaning." Classic three-phrase construction (it was called *tricolon* by the classical rhetoricians): "the landings and the beachheads and the details of the first two or three days. . . ." A contrast of high style ("a fleeting instant of heaven-sent tranquility") and plain style ("sweating out an enemy artillery or mortar barrage"). Contrast: "To the noncombatants . . ." vs. "to those who entered the meat grinder. . . ."

Sledge wasn't showing off, but he wasn't just blurting out the horrors of combat either. The final result is a prose which seems like the style Fussell describes. We all hunger for this kind of plain writing and plain truth. It runs especially deep in the American attitude toward language, but it has been expressed since the Greeks invented rhetoric. *Ars est celare artem,* as the Romans later memorialized the attitude; the best art is the art which conceals its art. The best style is the style which is never noticed as a style. It should be like a crystal goblet that shows off the rich burgundy it contains but never calls attention to itself. (I take this metaphor from Beatrice Warde, who used it to talk about style in typesetting.) When a style becomes opaque, when you look *at* it rather than looking *through* it, the schoolmarmly bell of reproach begins to ring.

On this fear that style should never show its hand has been built the fundamental judgmental scaffold for prose styles; styles that show should be hanged, styles that don't, that exhibit the honesty, simplicity, and modesty that Fussell praises should be pardoned and, if good enough, praised. Bad vs. Good. Easy to remember; easy to apply. *Everybody* buys it and retails it.

But there are problems with this pious rule. Let me start with the wineglass metaphor. The glass you drink a wine from does, connoisseurs argue, affect the taste of the wine. It certainly affects how you feel about the wine; pour Château Lafite Rothschild in a jelly glass and the wine will reproach you. Packages matter, prose style packages as much as any other.

There's a deeper problem. The Western program of teaching how to speak and write, the program of formal rhetoric, from the beginning aimed to develop an acute self-consciousness about words. If such self-consciousness is the ultimate sin, then the whole educational program in words has been pointed in the wrong direction from the beginning. That can't be true. Instead, we are told that, after you develop an acute self-consciousness about style, you apply it to your speaking and writing, but in a hidden way that nobody will notice— not even, when you are in the full spate of invention, you yourself. But is this really "success," this art which hides itself? Does it illustrate "honesty, simplicity, and modesty"? Quite the reverse. It is a formula for hypocrisy not honesty, complexity not simplicity, feigned modesty rather than the real thing.

And what really happens when you are reading such an artfully artless creation? If the art is not, *at some level,* perceived, how can it work? You must, *somehow* and *somewhere,* be aware of the art. What really happens, if you think about it for a minute, is not hard to see. This perception of the stylistic surface varies, fluctuates in both frequency and amplitude. As you read Homer, you "press the siege" as C. S. Lewis put it, but then you stop and notice how Homer has used the oral formulae on this occasion, how they work and why they are used just here. Sometimes this awareness is full—Wow! Look at how he describes this!—sometimes noticed in passing. And sometimes this oscillation is fast and sometimes slow.

When we say we "don't notice the style," we mean only that the particular oscillation succeeds for this work, and the kind of work this work is, and for us who read it. We're back to the problem with "clarity." Nobody will argue that it is a bad thing, but it is not a helpful descriptive category. It is simply a notice that, this time, things worked for us.

Yet another problem. We may speak instinctively, or have an instinct (I use the word in an imprecise way here, but 'twill serve) to learn language, given a chance to hear it, but nobody has ever argued thus for writing. It is learned behavior and by no means all cultures have learned it. Even Sledge, as unself-conscious a writer as Fussell claims, revised, had a little help from his friends, as his "Acknowledgments" acknowledge. We hunger for spontaneous utterance, for the "profuse strains of unpremeditated art" which Shelley found in a skylark. But we don't write with the instinctive outpouring Shelley's skylark could call upon. We have to learn how to write. How to apprentice ourselves to previous skylarks.

That necessity brings up one final problem with the "art which conceals art" cliché, and it's a big one. If you are trying to *teach* composition, and your ideal is an invisible one, it makes teaching it kind of hard. You can't hit what you can't see, and teaching it is even harder. Many teachers, unless they have been made to work their way through this conundrum, give up and start talking about the moral lessons contained in a particular passage.

This chapter was an effort to analyze this familiar, yet paradoxical and oxymoronic piece of proverbial wisdom, this everlasting self-contradictory advice to "Act Natural."

4 The Delights of Jargon

> Down with those who would refuse man the right to profes-
> sional speech.
>
> Christopher Sykes, *What U-Future?*

DEFINITION, SAMUEL JOHNSON reminds us in *Rambler 125,*
stands outside the province of man. "There is scarcely any
species of writing, of which we can tell what is its essence,
and what are its constituents." Imagination always outstrips
our distinctions.

To attempt a definition of *jargon* threatens unusual dan-
gers. Jargon bears a high and highly indignant moral charge,
for one thing, and it pervades America, for another. It usually
means, as the usage expert H. W. Fowler says in *Modern English Usage,* "talk that is considered both ugly sounding and
hard to understand." Another usage expert, Bergen Evans, reminds us that "jargon is a term of contempt and must be
used carefully." I use it more broadly to mean styles serving
special groups, interests, and activities. Its exclusively pejo-
rative flavor—it is often hard to understand because it wants
to be, and by holding us at arm's length adds offense to per-
plexity—blurs what it is, how it works, and why it arose.

No one can deny that America in our time has produced
the finest flowering of specialist gobbledegook the planet has
seen. Witness the bureaucratic mumblespeak in chapter 2.
American jargon is such fun to contemplate, so full of pompous self-satisfaction on the one hand and cynical, knowing,

ritual mystification on the other that description hardly knows where to begin. I choose, as in chapter 2, my own backyard, the university. Consider this passage. It comes from a famous study in sociological theory, *The Social System,* by a famous sociologist, Talcott Parsons:

An element of a shared symbolic system which serves as a criterion or standard for selection among the alternatives of orientation which are intrinsically open in a situation may be called a value. . . . But from this motivational orientation aspect of the totality of action it is, in view of the role of symbolic systems, necessary to distinguish a "value-orientation" aspect. This aspect concerns, not the meaning of the expected state of affairs to the actor in terms of his gratification-deprivation balance but the content of the selective standards themselves. The concept of value-orientations in this sense is thus the logical device for formulating one central aspect of the articulation of cultural traditions into the action system.

It follows from the derivation of normative orientation and the role of values in action as stated above, that all values involve what may be called a social reference. . . . It is inherent in an action system that action is, to use one phrase, "normatively oriented." This follows, as was shown, from the concept of expectations and its place in action theory, especially in the "active" phase in which the actor pursues goals. Expectations then, in combination with the "double contingency" of the process of interaction as it has been called, create a crucially imperative problem of order. Two aspects of this problem of order may in turn be distinguished, order in the symbolic systems which make communication possible, and order in the mutuality of motivational orientation to the normative aspect of expectations, the 'Hobbesian' problem of order.

The problem of order, and thus of the nature of the integration of stable systems of social interaction, that is, of social structure, thus focuses on the integration of the motivation of actors with the normative cultural standards which integrate the action system, in our context interpersonally. These standards are, in the terms used in the preceding chapter, patterns of value-orientation, and as such are a particularly crucial part of the cultural tradition of the social system.

Typical Parsons, and though not everyone has Parsons's talent for this kind of prose, many have emulated him. You wonder what it means? Fortunately, another sociologist of equal distinction though less orthodox profile, C. Wright Mills, after he has quoted the passage above, has translated it into English:

> People often share standards and expect one another to stick to them. In so far as they do, their society may be orderly. (*The Sociological Imagination,* pp. 25–27)

The social sciences increasingly provide the most popular majors in American universities. Students are being *taught* to write like this. Not, to be fair to most social scientists, taught directly. Not one in a thousand student papers in the social sciences is marked for style, up or down. But Parsons's kind of prose shines as an example. I came across a student in a composition class once who had actually been given a passage from Parsons on an examination. I asked her if she had understood it. What had she written as commentary? "Well, I couldn't figure out what it was about, you know, but, like, neither could the other kids, and I thought, like, they just wanted the same kind of bullshit back. So that's what I wrote. I got a B+." What kind of example had she been set? What does it exemplify?

First, it shows that the scientific ideal of clear, conceptual prose The Books dwell upon hasn't much application among working scientists. If you are a scientist, especially a social one, you had better *sound* scientific, the more scientific the better. Mills's clarity sounds so much less scientific than Parsons's sociologese. Mills's prose, clear, vigorous, sensible, the best plain prose of the scientific attitude, concentrates its energy on the subject. Parsons's prose aims to fix our gaze on the sociologist. What a wizard he must be to understand "motivational orientation aspect of the totality of action"— much less to pluck from such a nettle the rose, "value-orientation aspect." While the rest of us worry about "what other people will think," Parsons ponders that "it is inherent in an action system that action is, to use one phrase, 'normatively oriented.'" While we realize, after a couple of drinks, that society holds together because we mostly do what people expect us to, the social scientist perceives a deeper truth:

> The problem of order, and thus of the nature of the integration of stable systems of social interaction, that is, of social structure, thus focuses on the integration of the motivation of actors with the normative cultural standards which integrate the action system, in our context interpersonally.

Imagine an undergraduate who reads nothing but this. She learns, knowingly or not, an important lesson—but in hypocrisy not sociology: never say what you mean simply. It sounds *too* simple. The lesson will stand her in good stead later, when she joins the bureaucracy of her choice. For prose like this is largely an exercise in the presentation of self.

Parsons flatters Parsons. What he has to say about sociology can be said, as Mills points out, in twenty-five words or less. But he does not only flatter Parsons. He flatters all the sociologists who read him. What arcana they share! What bright chaps they must be to share them! Parsons's prose embarrasses us; coming from a teacher of the young, it should chill the blood. Only a strong hidden rhetoric could explain its appeal. Surely this rhetoric is the flattery, the ritual mystification that keeps the outsiders out and the insiders so pleased with themselves. We cannot condemn such prose as a failure. It has raised Parsons to wealth and honor; it has illuminated and refreshed innumerable social scientists of like mind. For them, it embodies clarity itself.

It works, then, because it works upon sociologists not upon society. It gives them a flattering image of themselves and this, for good prose in the world outside composition class, remains the essential ingredient. To the bright student, young and breathless, it unveils a mystery. With energy, pluck, and luck, he too can join this group. Self-flattery and ritual mystification make effective recruiting posters.

Such a prose style does not stop at creating an image of the sociologist; it depicts a society. Read the passage again. Do you notice the strings of prepositional phrases? In the one sentence just singled out: *of* order, *of* the nature *of* the integration *of* stable systems *of* social interaction, *of* social structure, *on* the integration, *of* the motivation *of* actors *with* the normative cultural standards, *in* our context. The man writes entirely with prepositional phrases, all dependent on one another. Such sentences can have no shape or rhythm, they simply lurch forward from one preposition to the next. More important, such sentences consist almost entirely of *nouns.* The example just cited poses one main verb, "focuses," and one subordinate one, "integrate." For the rest, heaps of the Latinate "-ion" terminology that sets the tone of sociologese: interaction, integration, motivation, action.

Verbs make things happen. To describe society with nouns rather than verbs implies the opposite of what (I think) Parsons wants to say. Here is a linguist on the noun-verb relationship:

> We often observe this contrast between the absence of nominal inflection and the richness of the verbal inflection. This is due to the nature of the noun and the verb. The noun indicates an idea of permanent nature: a thing, a person, or a quality; the verb indicates a process. . . . For the very reason that it indicates a permanent notion, the noun has a sole form or at most a principal form from which the others are derived. On the other hand, the verb, which indicates a process, has personal forms and the expression of nuances which vary with languages, but can be numerous. The fact that the forms of the noun and verb obey divergent tendencies thus results from the nature of things. (A. Meillet, *The Comparative Method in Historical Linguistics,* p. 114)

"Meaning," then, in the Parsons passage, tells the student that society is a process, "style," that society stands still. Likely to be confused by the terminology, if a student understands it he will become more so. Students learn the lessons such professional mystification teaches. If they are to join the system, they must learn to fool others—and more importantly to fool themselves—in precisely this way.

Even as students, they must swim in this pool of mystification daily. Consider this memo circulated by the dean of students at a large state university:

> During the 1969–1970 academic year, the [Frothingslosh U.] Student Services underwent a "participatory reconceptualization." The participating groups included many individuals from both senior and junior levels of staff. One of the many outcomes of the reconceptualization was the recommendation that a Pilot Decentralized Service Center be established for the 1970–1971 academic year. After some thought and discussion with various staff members, we have decided to implement the recommendation.

The dean, like Parsons, teaches an important lesson, and not only of prose.

Mystification for professional purposes is nothing new, of course. An orthopedic surgeon I recently came to know had just replaced a broken hip joint with a plastic one. "The prosthesis," he told me, "is in place." I was impressed. If he had said, discarding the Greek derivative, "the ball-and-socket is now glued in," he could not have charged $1500. Jargons aim to define situations in flattering ways, and we are, as often as not, included in the flattery. But, as in the surgeon's case, the flattery seldom affects the surgery. It is, like his secretary's white uniform, part of the flummery that tries to justify exorbitant fees.

In the academy, the flummery *becomes* the surgery. Students come to write like Parsons, and to think like Parsons. Here is an example of a first-rate student paper (it got an "A" and very kind words) in linguistics.

The authors state that the learning of two languages from childhood has favorable effects on the thinking process because, "By constantly hearing the same things referred to by different words from two languages the attention is drawn to the context (essentials) instead of form." (p. 3) Although this argument is based upon the idea that thought is dissociated from words, the authors seem to infer that mere word association between vocabularies of two languages encourages the bilingual child to conceptualize. My opinion is that having two language vocabularies does not lead to conceptual thinking. Mental flexibility arises from the bilingual's need to associate two languages' different grammatical constructions and idiomatic expressions and recognize that they refer to the same concepts.

A translation? "Learning two languages, the authors think, encourages a young child to think of concepts rather than words. I disagree. Grammatical and syntactical comparisons, much rather, stir him to think." The shapeless sentences, the flat, unemphatic assertion buried beneath a mound of *that*'s and prepositional phrases—here, the student is taught, shines the true face of science. And she is writing about language and its relationship to concepts, *about* the scientific attitude toward prose!

It would be comforting to think of social scientists as the barbarians of the future and literary critics as priests attendant on the gemlike flame. Here is how one critic writes to the London *Times Literary Supplement.* America cannot be blamed here; the writer is a Cambridge don:

Sir,—It is disappointing to find Professor Fuller, in his lecture on science and poetry (May 14), rehearsing the traditionally grave arguments against the integrity of Shelley's imaginative procedures only to concede with facile judiciousness, that the old case must still stand. For thirty-five years later we might perhaps distinguish two components in Dr. Leavis's analysis: that in the sequence of overt or implied metaphor or simile the initial ground for comparison from which the figure rises often has less primacy in the direction of later development than the new areas of reference introduced by the figure; and that this induces confusion and exemplifies a damaging central weakness of mind.

Whatever interesting detail is unearthed about the hitherto less closely observed niceties of scientific reference in Shelley's vocabulary, the justice of the first component in this analysis cannot be disputed, and indeed it was a brilliantly shrewd piece of attentiveness to the uncongenial. What we may doubt is whether the second stage of the diagnosis *necessarily* follows from the first; and if not necessarily, then whether in a range of important particular cases it seems actually to describe our critical response. For we can by now surely see why, assuming on prior moral-epistemic grounds a *necessary* entailment, Dr. Leavis could hardly make dispassionate critical appraisal of the actualities. (May 28, 1971)

Literary Parsonsese. The terms of art observe a higher tone and do not so often break the jaw—"imaginative procedures, of acute judiciousness, sequence of overt or implied metaphor or simile, less primacy in the direction of later development, damaging central weakness of mind," and later, "variable transfer of the criteria for imaginative coherence, overlapping figurational transformation." But the same aesthetic prevails. The critic walls out *hoi polloi,* stages himself within as verbal magician, witch-doctor of words. Of course he may actually think this way. "Literary education,"

Northrop Frye reminds us in *The Well-Tempered Critic,* "should lead not merely to the admiration of great literature, but to some possession of its power of utterance" (p. 47). This is obviously not the case here, and is not usually so, at least in America.

Literary education seems to make no difference at all to the utterance of most students passing through it. In conversation, the student of literature displays the same spastic drool of *likes, you knows,* and *wows* that disfigure his mates in sociology and physics. His prose crawls with the same painful spasms. No discipline is exempt; only a few sin egregiously. Beyond the academy walls, the same flapdoodle is retailed, the retailers being less culpable since, though the young are betrayed, the betrayers do not masquerade as teachers.

We are, clearly enough, deep into the moral attitude toward prose. Confronted with Parsons's prose, it is hard to keep perspective. For students, it must be hard to keep a balanced mind. Imagine one hour spent reading Shakespeare's sonnets, and the next with this:

When the integrated part of the mind has been distorted in a bygone period by an unusual splitting off of those aspects of established functions which precipitated experiences of overwhelming disorganization or unpleasure as they were being increasingly utilized by normally emerging instinctual drive representatives, then the split-off portion can be regarded as a surviving representative of instinctual operations responsible for the formation or the maintenance of phase-specific mental organization. (Theodore Lipin, "Sensory Irruptions and Mental Organization," *Journal of the American Psychoanalytic Association,* vol. 17, no. 4)

No wonder students begin to feel schizzy. Change classes, change worlds.

Inevitable—and enjoyable—as the moral attitude is toward mumblespeak, such an attitude offers neither remedy nor pedagogy. Plenty of people deplore-with-grave-concern the jargon scene. But moralizing offers no way out. It will not reform professors who fool their students with mumbo jumbo. It will not keep bureaucrats from playing variations on "That's not my department." It will not commit to truth a politician aiming to commit himself to nothing, or prohibit university presidents from marketing exuberant inanities. Jargons, like other styles, respond to situations. To prevent them, we must change the situation. Freshman Composition will not bring such a change. Moralizing composition teachers pray that if you get the cant out of someone's prose, you will get the cant out of his mind. No evidence supports such optimism. Once again, what to do? Give up? No. Give in.

I was once sitting in a faculty meeting listening to the mumblespeak fall like gentle rain. A new colleague, fresh to the scene and, worse, an Englishman, whispered in my ear, "My God, is it always like this?" It is. But I surprised myself. I was not offended by the mumblespeak, I was enjoying it. I was simultaneously translating it into English, trying—purely as one Anthropoid Input, of course—to guess between whose shoulder blades the next "ongoing reappraisal" would strike, praying for an "incremental adjustment" (raise in salary), keeping a five-count—a long-standing habit—of "the fact that" and "like you know." Nonsense turned into game. Such an epiphany did not fail of pedagogical implication. I could not metamorphose the speaker into a sensible man, supply a sense of humor, inject a liberal education. No more can a student cut off the daily flow of jargon he drowns in. But he can be taught to recognize it, see through it, even laugh at it. If you cannot reform nonsense, you may learn to banquet off it. For this, the moral attitude helps.

First, you must translate jargon into English. But the job only begins here. You must also understand what situation a jargon responds to, how it works. Learn the languages. The desired result seems that yielded by foreign language study—reflection on the nature of language itself, the limitations it imposes on our knowing and expressing. More than this, another language pleases in itself. Even a mumblespeak supplies a new conceptual world, complete with intriguing bafflements and charming mysteries. To survive in a world of mumblespeaks, use the comparative method, become a connoisseur. This is no unhopeful thing, as we shall see. The connoisseur strategy is an old one but promises to flourish again now. Starting with an old and famous example of such stylistic debunking, we move to several modern instances.

The oldest jargon, if poetry really did precede prose historically, is the language of poetry, "poetic diction." Not usually ugly, grasping no *parti pris* advantage, it exists—as all jargons finally do—for pleasure. Alexander Pope, in attacking the poetic diction of his day, employed the exemplary strategy for dealing with jargon. His title parodies Longinus's treatise on sublimity and its high style ("*Peri Hupsous:* The Art of Soaring in Poetry") in "*Peri Bathous:* The Art of Sinking in Poetry." His essay creates its stylistic comedy by applying a scientific attitude to an opaque style. Such should be the fundamental strategy for dealing with jargon. Not moral reproach but translation and imitation best create comic awareness. Here are some of Pope's translations:

> Who knocks at the Door?
> For whom thus rudely pleads my loud-tongued gate,
> That he may enter? . . .
> See who is there?
> Advance the fringed curtains of thy eyes,
> And tell me who comes yonder . . .
> Shut the Door.
> The wooden guardian of our privacy
> Quick on its axle turn . . .
> Bring my Clothes.
> Bring me what Nature, tailor to the Bear,
> To Man himself denied: She gave me Cold,
> But would not give me Clothes . . .
> Light the Fire.
> Bring forth some remnant of Promethean theft,
> Quick to expand th'inclement air congealed
> By Boreas' rude breath . . .
> Snuff the candle.
> Yon Luminary amputation needs,
> Thus shall you save its half-extinguished life.
> Open the Letter.
> Wax! render up thy trust . . .
> Uncork the Bottle, and chip the Bread.
> Apply thine engine to the spongy door,
> Set Bacchus from his glassy prison free,
> And strip white Ceres of her nut-brown coat.

Jargon's wellspring stands exposed—to flatter ordinary reality. Pope, no more than C. Wright Mills, pauses over this flattery. Both see jargon only as the last stage in stylistic disinte-gration. True enough, in Pope's day and ours. But might not our jargon explosion be an encouraging sign, too?

Moralistic critics of jargon see it as corrupting, mali-ciously or mindlessly, a preexistent scientific clarity. They consider it what the Latin rhetoricians called a *color*, a strat-egy to present your case in its most favorable light. We began this chapter by varying such a theme. But even sociologese deserves a kindlier gaze. In the first place, necessity often de-mands a terminology. Unless continually redefined, it must seem arcane. However stupefying its sound to an outsider, familiarity renders it agreeable to cognoscenti. Familiarity creates clarity. But beyond need and rhetorical or psycholog-ical advantage lies the fun of a special language. Amidst the moral disapproval of jargon as debasing the means of con-scious life, no one has noticed that jargons are fun—and not simply to their connoisseur but to their user, self-conscious or not.

People seldom content themselves with plain utterance even in daily life. It gets boring. They invent tautological and periphrastic equivalents to relieve the tedium. They prefer the metaphorical, the indirect expression to the straight-forward, literal one. They are not trying to be literary. Meta-phors are just more fun. With stylized phrases, all kinds of attitudes, feelings, in-jokes come to life—a whole range of expressivity that scientific prose excludes. Here the cliché was begotten—for pleasure—by Variety on Familiarity. Frank Sullivan illustrated this surprising paternity in an immortal *New Yorker* piece (August 31, 1935) called "The Cliché Ex-pert Takes the Stand."

Q—Mr. Arbuthnot, you are an expert in the use of the cliché, are you not?

A—Yes, sir, I am a certified public cliché expert.

Q—In that case would you be good enough to answer a few questions on the use and application of the cliché in ordinary speech and writing?

A—I should be only too glad to do so.

Q—Thank you. Now, just for the record—you live in New York?

A—I like to visit New York but I wouldn't live here if you gave me the place.

Q—Then where do you live?

A—Any old place I hang my hat is home sweet home to me.

Q—What is your age?

A—I am fat, fair, and forty.

Q—And your occupation?

A—Well, after burning the midnight oil at an institution of higher learning, I was for a time a tiller of the soil. Then I went down to the sea in ships for a while, and later, at various times, I have been a guardian of the law, a gentleman of the Fourth Estate, a poet at heart, a bon vivant and raconteur, a prominent clubman and man about town, an eminent—

Q—Just what is your occupation at the moment, Mr. Arbuthnot?

A—At the moment I am an unidentified man of about forty, shabbily clad.

Q—Now then, Mr. Arbuthnot, what kind of existence do you, as a cliché expert, lead?

A—A precarious existence.

Q—And what do you do to a precarious existence?

A—I eke it out.

Q—Have you ever been in a kettle of fish?

A—Oh, yes.

Q—What kind?

A—A pretty kettle of fish.

Q—How do you cliché experts reveal yourselves, Mr. Arbuthnot?

A—In our true colors, of course.

Q—And you expect to live to . . .

A—A ripe old age.

Q—What do you shuffle off?

A—This mortal coil.

Q—What do you thank?

A—My lucky stars.

Q—What kind of retreats do you like?

A—Hasty retreats.

Q—What do you do to hasty retreats?

A—I beat them.

Clichés are petrified metaphors. The moralist stresses the petrified, berates stale language, and, if a critic, numbers the blessings of poetry. Poetry, by putting language under pressure in new verbal environments, creates it anew, refreshes it, invents new metaphors or, like Sullivan, galvanizes the clichés with irony. Stress the *metaphor* and we see jargon begin. Clichés work paradoxically, as a generally shared specialist language (special to situations, not speakers). They develop from the pleasures we take in language. They live in the play impulse, the play attitude toward style. They are often ironized, "super-enclichéd," before the essayist embraces them. So we say not "Oh, I can make myself comfortable anywhere" but "Any old place I hang my hat is home sweet home to me." "Home sweet home" provides a nicely domestic cliché to bounce your freedom against, and hanging your hat is a human gesture, not a concept like "making yourself at home." We've all done it—or did it when people wore hats—

and can enhance it with a whole vocabulary of gestures and attitudes. In Stendhal's definition, it has style, action, plus circumambient attitudes.

If, at forty, we say "I am forty, slightly overweight, but quite contented with life, thank you very much," we are clear, as The Books demand, but miss the pleasures of alliteration. If we have studied at a university, then farmed, then sailed the seas, we may say so thus. But such a statement, to be applauded for its clarity, its avoidance (how The Books dwell on this) of cliché, has no past. If we burn the midnight oil, we tread in the footsteps of Horace; if we till the soil, our tilth has biblical precedent. And being in an "uncomfortable situation" can hardly compare to a warm and companionable kettle of fish. When it is all over, who would simply die when he could, with comfy panache, kick the bucket? Such expressions are fun to tease because they were fun to begin with. They illustrate man's natural flight from plain statement, from the scientific to the play attitude toward style.

Jargon is like rhetoric. It always describes what the *other* guy does. We argue, he indulges in specious rhetoric. We make ourselves clear, he speaks jargon. All of us languish in the grip of the scientific attitude. Unwilling to grant the other fellow his pleasures, we cannot forego our own. We might see more clearly would we acknowledge—and develop—our common pleasure in words. As Kenneth Burke wrote on eloquence in *Counter-Statement:*

> The primary purpose of eloquence is not to enable us to live our lives on paper—it is to convert life into its most thorough verbal equivalent. The categorical appeal of literature resides in a liking for verbalization as such, just as the categorical

appeal of music resides in a liking for musical sounds as such. (p. 167)

We feel an irrepressible urge to render our experience literary, metaphorical, scaled to and intimately involved with man. We want to render it, not clear and scientific, but rich, human, full of indirection. Burke discusses the pressure within a literary work to intricate itself "until in all its smallest details the work bristles with disclosures, contrasts, restatements with a difference, ellipses, images, aphorism, volume, sound-values, in short all that complex wealth of minutiae which in their line-for-line aspect we call style" (*Counter-Statement,* p. 38).

We must learn to think of jargon thus kindly, as an effort toward style. Our current tidal wave of it may well be created by our national effort to be clear, to write prose exclusively under the scientific rubric. The need for style thus rushes in through the back door of jargon, disheveled and dirty, unprepossessing, but testifying to an ancient hunger. Another kind of book might pause to anatomize American bad taste, explaining it, in the same way, as the play attitude's response to an overstressed scientific attitude toward style. For prose, the lesson stands plain. If you aim only at a scientific style, you will end up with a bad style, with ugly jargon and comic debunking as the only corrective. The wave of jargon, testifying to an unsatisfied love of words, a starved play attitude toward style, may presage a countercycle.

Jargon, then, can gesture toward belonging, toward social solidarity. It can present a version of self. It can play.

Added up, these constitute something like the opaque style discussed earlier. Jargon yields that stylistic self-consciousness shared by reader and writer which renders style a subject, an acknowledged way of looking at the world. Jargon always moves in this direction; however *lumpen,* it approaches the lightness of play. Ample illustration of this movement has been provided by frequent *spoofs* of the computerized and militarized government jargon called bureaucratese. One of them begins:

> After a recent Vietnam bombing mission, a B-52 pilot summed up the day's work as an "effective ordnance delivery" (translation: target demolished). When George Romney abruptly exited from the Presidential race, his New Hampshire campaign manager explained that the candidate believed he lacked "a positive reference input" (translation: a good image). In its January letter to shareholders, Litton Industries attributed declining stock profits to "volume variances from plan" (translation: strikes).
>
> Once confined to Mad Ave and Foggy Bottom, euphemisms, circumlocutions, jargon and other high-flown forms of linguistic obfuscation have now become as pervasive as pollution. From San Antonio (where the sidewalks at HemisFair are called "people expressways") to New York City (where a garage mechanic advertises himself as an "automotive internist"), the word is out that anything goes verbalizationwise.
>
> Physicians are starting to call pep pills "activity boosters." A Milwaukee brokerage house recently touted a certain stock because it had "a small downside risk with a worthwhile upside potential." Preschoolers are now enrolled in "early learning centers," where they orbit between their "pupil stations" (desks) and the "instructional materials resource center" (library). ("New Peak for Newspeak," *Newsweek,* May 6, 1968)

Even from behind so moral, so grisly a context, the spirit of play peeps out. It does so still more in the game, "How to win at wordsmanship," appended to the article:

> After years of hacking through etymological thickets at the U.S. Public Health Service, a 63-year-old official named Philip Broughton hit upon a sure-fire method for converting frustration into fulfillment (jargonwise). Euphemistically called the Systematic Buzz Phrase Projector, Broughton's system employs a lexicon of 30 carefully chosen "buzzwords":

Column 1	Column 2	Column 3
0. integrated	0. management	0. options
1. total	1. organizational	1. flexibility
2. systematized	2. monitored	2. capability
3. parallel	3. reciprocal	3. mobility
4. functional	4. digital	4. programming
5. responsive	5. logistical	5. concept
6. optional	6. transitional	6. time-phase
7. synchronized	7. incremental	7. projection
8. compatible	8. third-generation	8. hardware
9. balanced	9. policy	9. contingency

> The procedure is simple. Think of any three-digit number, then select the corresponding buzzword from each column. For instance, number 257 produces "systematized logistical projection," a phrase that can be dropped into virtually any report with that ring of decisive, knowledgeable authority. "No one will have the remotest idea of what you're talking about," says Broughton, "but the important thing is that they're not about to admit it."

Here we jump wholly into the game sphere, into that childlike state that puts words together for the fun of it, freeing them from the need to make sense. Notice how all the words in the game are scientific? Scientific prose, pushed as far as it will go, turns into a game. The ends of the spectrum meet to make it a circle.

As relief from the straight society's jargon we might, like many others, lust after hippie delights. The hip world has deliberately cultivated a second language. Modeled originally on the argot of the black ghetto, it has been taken over for just the reasons that all jargons are devised, to protect a group, enhance its sense of identity, express the concepts peculiar to it, and to have fun. Several glossaries of hip talk have been compiled to guide the straights. Here is the one in Lewis Yablonsky's brilliant and humane study, *The Hippie Trip:*

Bag: a personal area of involvement or interest, as in "that's his bag"

Behind-it: sincerely committed to a particular subject of action

Bread: money

Bug: bother, annoy

Bummer: an emotionally unpleasant or upsetting experience; also, a negative drug reaction, as an "LSD bummer"

Burned: cheated

Busted: arrested

Clark Kent hippies: part-timers who live mainly in straight society; week-end hippies

Cop-out: to confess, or to compromise one's position or beliefs

Cool: to be tuned-in, into things

Cut out: leave

Dig: enjoy, appreciate, understand

Far out: unusual, extraordinary; bizarre or avant-garde

Flash-on: to think about; become intensely aware of or
   remember
Freak-out: to lose control, to have bizarre patterns of thought
   or behavior. Often occurring under the influence of a
   drug
Grass: marijuana
Groove: to "swing," to enjoy, to be "with it"
Hassle: an annoyance or a conflict situation
Head: a frequent user of psychedelic drugs, as in acid-head
   or pot-head
Heat: police
Hip: to be "in," "with it," emotionally wise, in the know
Joint: marijuana cigaret
Man (the): police; or drug dealer
Out front: open; honest; or the preface to a statement
Out of sight: so good that words fail to describe it
Rap: to talk; or present one's particular point of view
Roach: butt of a marijuana cigaret
Spade: a Negro. Used in a non-discriminatory way
Split: to leave
Square: a person or thing, not tuned-in or in the know
Stoned: very high on drugs
Teenybopper: a teenage "plastic" hippie
Turn-on: to use a drug; to get into the new scene
Up-tight: overly anxious or nervous (pp. 367–68)

This jargon, though not without its nightmares, its bad-trip-
ping speed freaks who never come down, seems a charm and
a delight compared to bureaucratic mumblespeak. The reasons are not far to seek. It does not try to be scientific. Like
the movement it enshrines, it grounds itself in feelings, not
concepts, in metaphor, in the play attitude, not the scientific
or moral ones. The glossary cited is pure metaphor, folk

poetry, cliché being born. (The terms may solidify into ironic cliché in the hip world, as they have already done outside. "Right on!" for the straights now signifies a heavily ironic approval.)

A comparison of sociological or governmental mumble-speak with hip talk carries us deep into the social problems that bedevil us. Mumblespeak aims above all to sound impersonal, conceptual. It is not *written,* it precipitates out of a committee: "It was decided that," "a significant implementation was effected." It gets as far away as it can from people and their unashamedly metaphorical attempts to cope with the world. It masquerades as inevitable historical process. It waddles concept-heavy, obese with nouns. Notice, in the hip glossary, how many verbs there are? How many expressions —*high, up front, behind it*—imply movement or physical location? How close the terms stay to basic realities of human life? The bureaucrat speaks of the "appropriate regulatory authorities," the hippie of "the heat."

Let us try a more extended example. Here are two discussions of sex. The first, from an article entitled "Voluntary Control of Eroticism" (Donald E. Henson and H. B. Rubin, *Journal of Applied Behavior Analysis,* vol. 4, 1972, no. 1), investigates, you see at last, whether men watching dirty movies can voluntarily avoid having an erection:

> Laws and Rubin (1961) reported that penile erection, an autonomic visceral response (Kelly, 1961) that is generally considered involuntary . . . could be voluntarily controlled by normal male subjects. Their subjects were able both to produce erections in the absence of erotic stimuli and inhibit erections in the presence of effective erotic stimulation. Each

subject reported that tumescence was achieved by "fantasizing" about erotic events, and that inhibition was accomplished by producing competing stimuli, i.e., concentrating on asexual stimuli. . . .

Since the attending indicator of the Laws and Rubin study (1969) ensured attendance only to the display area of the erotic stimulation, the contention can be made that their subjects were not attending to the content of the stimuli when voluntary inhibition occurred. However, if penile inhibition is possible when attendance to the content of erotic stimulation is guaranteed, then it must be assumed that the automatic visceral response of penile erection can be at least partially modified by voluntary controls.

METHOD

Subjects

Eight adult males (age 21 to 30 yrs.) volunteered to serve as subjects. Two (S-1 and S-2) were employees of Anna State Hospital, had participated in an earlier study . . . , and received no remuneration. Three subjects (S-3, S-4, and S-5) were experimentally naive, were students at Southern Illinois University, and were remunerated for their transportation and time at the rate of $2.50 per hour.

The remaining three subjects did not complete the study, two because during their baseline test session, sample stimulus films were ineffective in eliciting full penile erection, and the third because he attempted to control his penile erection by manipulating his penis. All subjects were fully informed of the nature of the experiment.

For contrast, here is an East Village hippie describing the sexual customs of that scene:

> There are girls around here that hit on guys—two or three different guys a day sometimes. It's much freer here. When

you are in a group and you and a girl want to ball and there are some guys with you and you want to get rid of them, you don't try to explain to them. Like if you were at school or something, you know, like "Would you do us a favor—go out and get us some ice cream or something?" But here you just say, "Now look, I'm going in that room and that room is the 'ball room,' you know, I'm going to do 'my thing,' excuse me for a while." The way it is back home, everybody knows that girls are getting screwed and that guys are having a good time. I mean, everybody knows that. Ninety-five percent of the girls in the school I went to were not virgins. Everybody knows that. But the first time that the fact comes out that a girl has been screwed in school, automatically she becomes a whore. Here it is different. Like I mean, back home there are lots of girls getting screwed in school, you know, and everybody secretively knows it. But the first time somebody comes along and says, "Hey, Mary got screwed last night," everybody starts on the big thing that Mary is a whore. Now here, like Mary got screwed last night and she went and did it, well, gee whiz, good enough—wow, I mean what's it to me? I mean, wow, that's the way it is here. (Yablonsky, *The Hippie Trip*, pp. 121–22)

No point in talking about which style is *better*. Both make us laugh. The first, preoccupied with a subject that creates ribaldry almost spontaneously, bends over backwards to keep a scientific straight face. In fact, the authors create delightful stylistic comedy. Content and style stand so far apart in this prose that the ordinary reader (though not, I suppose, the social scientist) responds, as the experiment progresses from stage to humorless stage, with burgeoning laughter. If the authors had written the experiment up in ordinary prose, of course, no journal would have published it—no status trip. Plain language would not have made the prose less scientific, but it would have *seemed* so. Hence the jargon.

The hippie's explanation of ballroom etiquette, by contrast, stays close to the surface of experience. Not scientific—a social scientist would write "fornicatorium" not "ball room" —it is direct, immediate, intensely metaphorical. Compared to the "Voluntary Control of Eroticism," it lives, that's all. It would be a mistake to call it a plain style. It gets down to facts through *metaphor.* For example, take that most delicate of all problems, words for the sex act. English, let alone American, has no word that simply expresses sexual intercourse without implying an attitude. *Screw* is lewd, *make love* euphemistic, *fornicate* biblical, *copulate* clinical, *fuck* vulgar. So one is devised: *to ball.* A new expression for a new attitude toward sex. Could sociologists capable of the mumblespeak we have just read ever develop the stylistic awareness needed to see the changing social attitudes behind "you and a girl want to ball"?

The hip jargon here quoted is, like all hippie jargon, hip *talk.* You cannot imagine anyone ever *speaking or reading aloud,* "Voluntary Control of Eroticism." It is unreadable. Consequently, it possesses no rhythm, no life. It is otherwise with young Brian (age eighteen) chronicling hippie sex. Read the passage aloud. You catch intonation and stress immediately. Part of American tone-deafness has been an addiction to a pitchless monotone. Change in pitch is natural to hippie talk, just as it is to black speech. Change in pitch, in fact, often signifies change in meaning. As in any limited vocabulary (and hip-talk has a very limited vocabulary) one word serves many uses. Listen to a dozen *out of sight*'s or *too much*'s. You'll notice that pitch makes meaning. This creates a speech more agreeable to listen to.

Northrop Frye calls such rhythm "associative" and thinks the habits of hippie speech are corruptions of it. Endless interruptions of *like* and *you know,* utterance begun and left hanging, betoken an ego running free, out of control. (See chapter 2, "Manual of Style," in *The Well-Tempered Critic.*) He is surely right, and yet, in the passage we have, don't we see, too, a hunger for style, for a style closer to experience than the scientific attitude allows? Like everything else in the hippie world, hip jargon adumbrates problems in the straight world. What surfaces here is dissatisfaction with the remote inhumanity, the impersonality of journalistic reporting, of mumblespeak, of the preposterous drivel that politicians talk.

An example of this last is President Nixon's First Inaugural Address:

> I ask you to share with me today the majesty of this moment. In the orderly transfer of power, we celebrate the unity that keeps us free.
>
> Each moment in history is a fleeting time, precious and unique. But some stand out as moments of beginning, in which courses are set that shape decades or centuries.
>
> This can be such a moment.
>
> Forces now are converging that make possible, for the first time, the hope that many of man's deepest aspirations can at last be realized. The spiraling pace of change allows us to contemplate, within our own lifetime, advances that once would have taken centuries.
>
> In throwing wide the horizons of space, we have discovered new horizons on earth.

For the first time, because the people of the world want peace, and the leaders of the world are afraid of war, the times are on the side of peace.

Eight years from now America will celebrate its 200th anniversary as a nation. Within the lifetime of most people now living, mankind will celebrate that great new year which comes only once in a thousand years—the beginning of the third millennium.

What kind of a nation we will be, what kind of a world we will live in, whether we shape the future in the image of our hopes, is ours to determine by our actions and our choices.

Prose like this renders suspect all words except the fundamental ones. So you use those over and over. At least they don't share the taint of patent hypocrisy that public prose like this drags in from "the plastic world" (another hip metaphor).

Hippie talk succeeds in recreating their world for people who don't know it firsthand. We should not, however, sentimentalize it. The stock responses, the simplistic opinions, the persistent, pure mindlessness of the hippie trip, come through loud and clear. But their language does shine with life and humor. Mumblespeak, equally expressive of its milieu, offers neither. Both jargons "work." A comparison must choose, not styles but worlds, life-styles, ways to live.

For diversion, imagine young Brian in Freshman Composition. Most composition teachers, in fact, do not need to imagine him at all. He'll be—or probably not be—in class tomorrow. The topic for the day: "What I Did Last Summer." So Brian tells all. It comes out as above. What to do? The Books, of course, all have a section on jargon. It's probably called, in the schematic end-paper *index errorum*, "Jarg." The

Books are not having any Jargs. If you are Walter Scott and a Scot and writing about Scottish conversation, maybe you can try Jarg, if you call it "Dial." Otherwise not. The Books can't cope with Brian's style because Brian's *attitude* toward style does not figure in their stylistic universe. Try to normalize it according to the scientific attitude, and it vanishes. Yet it is not fiction. It is actual conversation, transcribed from a tape (and surely this is how some students now write their "papers"). It is genuinely comic, not, like "Voluntary Eroticism," unintentionally so. In any sense in which the phrase means anything, it "has style." Yet it is clearly a jargon and contaminated with the worst associative rhythms, the *like* and *you know* speech disease.

"Scientific language," a well-known linguist tells us, "tends to surmount language, so as to overcome the vernacular, and to become universal" (Joshua Whatmough, *Language,* p. 102). Hip talk constitutes a plea for the vernacular and the pleasures of jargon at the same time. It is not without pedagogical implications. Any scheme of prose style that does not have room for it and styles like it—and not simply room to condemn—should be scrapped. Stylistic experience constitutes a full continuum. It is never turned off. We should be able to make sense of—ideally, to relish—any style, especially those which surround us. A scheme that can describe Sir Thomas Browne's "Urn-Burial" but not Brian's disquisition on balling is worse than useless. Worse, because it reinforces the worst of American errors, the delusion that style is only for poetry, for the classroom, not for—and part of—everyday life.

The obvious therapy is not only to normalize jargons but to imitate them, parody them, and translate them one into another. America possesses no central normative prose style considered that of an educated person, no BBC English. We haven't the social structure a normative style emerges from and is built upon. Americans are born eclectics, in prose as in every other kind of style. Why not make the most of it?

Afterthoughts

THIS CHAPTER WAS an extended meditation on a central theme: If you kick style out the front door, it will creep in the back. Jargons are all written in the name of "clarity." A special field demands a special language. But once safely behind this professional fence, the special language grows ever more dense, ever more exclusive, grows so fond of itself that it begins to play, and then to veer off into self-parody. Practitioners write more and more for one another and for the pleasure of using the special terminology. We can simply condemn this—and I have done so—but you can learn more if you play games with it.

The *Anti-Textbook* is first and last a plea for pleasure in words. Such a plea was, when it first appeared, uphill work, and has become more so since. Since I wrote, professional languages have proliferated and become yet more dense. Yet a counter-pressure is at work. As Peter Drucker has written, a knowledge society "demands for the first time in history that people with knowledge take responsibility for making themselves understood by people who do not have the same knowledge base." It looked for a while as if the Common Reader of yore had died, but the need to convince those outside your professional language of the importance of what you do has resurrected this audience. Especially if you need money to pursue your professional purposes, or simply to be left in peace to pursue them. And occasionally scholars write for a general audience. Very occasionally, graduate departments offer a special course in how to write for an audience *outside* of your specialty.

The kind of translational play I recommend here seems to me more needed than ever. I was tempted to exchange the examples I used for more contemporary ones, but no purpose would be served by doing so. Nothing, really, has changed, and the original examples prove it. Translational play is, after all, a very old idea. Roman rhetoric, so much of which remains in use today, was a *bilingual* education: it was always looking back to Greece and Greek, and moving from Latin to Greek and back. As Latin developed into the Romance languages, the Latin provided the referential language and the evolving languages the second one. Movement back and forth was continual. The "grammar" Shakespeare learned was Latin grammar but the texts he learned from were translated into English and then back into Latin. The result was the kind of stylistic self-consciousness I recommend in this chapter, and from this self-consciousness came the deep pleasure in words for their own sake which Shakespeare's plays embody and which this book recommends.

5 Poetic Prose

The way to a man's heart is through his ears.
Xerxes, in Herodotus 7.39

MOST THEORISTS AGREE with The Books that, whatever a prose style should be, it cannot be "poetic." By this many things are meant. Prose cannot let its style show—in other words, cannot employ an opaque style. It cannot use the obvious rhetorical figures of sound and arrangement. It cannot allow style to become subject. It must express its subject but not change it by the mode of expression. A poem exists for its own sake, it serves itself. Prose must never do this. As Sir Herbert Read epigrammatizes it (*English Prose Style,* p. ix), "Poetry is creative expression: prose is constructive expression." The two modes of expression reflect two fundamentally different ways of thinking: "Poetry is the expression of one form of mental activity. Prose is the expression of another form." Prose is loyal to concepts, poetry to image, to itself. In a poem, writes the linguist Roman Jakobson, the coding interests us more than the message.

Reversing that definition fits it nicely to prose—in prose, the message predominates. Prose belongs to the intellect, poetry to the emotions. As Murry writes in *The Problem of Style:*

> The specific virtue of prose is that it is judicial; and that is a virtue that poetry cannot have: if it has, it is not poetry, but prose in metre. Where the appeal is to the judgement, there

the vehicle is prose: if the appeal is made with absolute economy, so that the movement is swift and certain to the conclusion, then it will give an aesthetic pleasure over and above its
convincing force. (pp. 60–61)

Metrical form does not separate prose from poetry, nor does
density of metaphorical language. The nature of the appeal,
the part of man's nature addressed, is what governs. An over-
plus of energy and effect, the job very well done, supplies a
bonus that is aesthetic but fortuitous. Loyalty must incline
to concept and conceptual intelligence. Murry makes the distinction historical: "Why was prose developed, if not to afford expression to a content which suffered by being thrust
into metrical form?" (p. 49). Such a distinction turns on our
three attitudes toward style—scientific, moral, and playful.
Once again, the playful, or aesthetic, ingredient must linger
outside the walls. This is poetry's domain. Information and
the moral censor that verifies it must animate prose.

The trouble with this definition is the worst trouble a
definition can have. It ignores most of the *definiendum,* the
thing to be defined. It defines, in its purity, only mathe-
matics. And it confuses students of literature, beginning and
professional, to the last degree. Description rather than definition seems in order. We may view any utterance with any
one of the three attitudes, or any combination of them. We
may read poetry for the story and thus invoke the scientific
attitude by demanding information. An experienced bureaucrat may search a conference report for minute hints of attitude, less for what was said than for how old Charley said
it, whether old Charley's head would roll and his replace it.
The prose may be vintage mumblespeak, but he, alert to

symbol and metaphor, will read it as poetry, for attitude and feeling.

Nobody can—and nobody should—make rules about what prose can do. It can do anything language can do. To say that if it does certain things it becomes poetry confuses us to no purpose. Reference to the non-invidious stylistic spectrum makes more sense and works as well for poetry as for prose. To what extent is style an issue? How self-conscious is the reader-writer relationship? Such a locating tool, easy and informative, spares us the agonies of redefinition required to distinguish fictional prose from nonfictional. The traditional scientific and moral definitions of prose obviously do not apply to fictional prose, so it must be poetry. And what about a prose that is fictional but reportorial? The whole definition collapses into such conundrums. Fictional prose is simply prose where the play attitude, the formal expectation, figures as strongly as the scientific expectation, sometimes more so. "Poetic" prose—fictional or not—simply moves further over on the spectrum.

No fundamental difference separates fictional from non-fictional prose, just as none divides prose and poetry. Any attitude, or combination of attitudes, may inform either pair, although perhaps the scientific attitude most often informs nonfictional prose. But to say so, you must do two things seldom done: read the prose carefully with the play attitude to see how the form works, and survey all the prose that has ever been written. The statement demands, and lends itself, at least theoretically, to quantitative proof. When critics say prose most often conveys information, they mean they usually read prose for information, and of course they find what they seek. Agree that the scientific attitude should prevail, and so it will. The pontificating task-force master quoted in an earlier chapter suffers acutely from the scientific attitude. He wears it like blinders. He cannot see how his utterance betrays his character. He sees information; the audience sees a donkey. The only therapy can be the active presence of all three attitudes.

Can no distinction, then, be made between prose and poetry? The only obvious one stares us in the face—the typographical one. And this amounts, finally, to signifying an appropriate attitude toward the reader. You arrange words in a certain linear pattern. This tells the reader the formal attitude is appropriate. To find to what degree it fits, one must read on. But the point is clear: poetic typography invites an attitude toward style. Few critics now contend that such an arrangement demands a certain subject, that poetry must treat a poetic subject. But most students of prose still insist that absence of this typographical arrangement *does* bring with it a certain subject matter. Poetry does not have an intrinsically poetic subject, but prose must have an intrinsically prosaic one. No fair.

To experiment, I look up at the bookshelves above my desk for the most "prosaic" book there. Dictionaries excluded, the choice falls on Goodwin and Gulick's *Greek Grammar.* In the *sortes virgilianae* manner, I open it by chance to page 312, a discussion of indirect discourse:

In
     direct Dis   course or Or
     ati-   o Ob
     liqua

A direct   quotation
        or   question gives   the exact words
of the original speaker
        or   writer.
In an in direct   quotation
                        or   question   the original words
    conform   to the
    construction   of the
    sentence   in which   they are
    quoted.

What's happening? The typography forces the play attitude
on a piece of authentically scientific prose. The similarity in
shape of "Indirect" and "A direct" is enforced by putting
them on different lines. The *o* vowel sounds (-or-Or o-Ob)
are pointed to by typographical clustering; so, too, *-ati-* and
-liqua- for *a* sounds. "Quotation" and "question" begin with
the same letter, and similarly, and contain nearly the same
number of syllables. So they go together. *In-an-in* makes a
nice sound play and so that gets isolated. And we want to pile
up the nouns that matter, those that form the passage's center. So we do that typographically too, stacking them up. And
the exact words and *the original words* earn a separate group-
ing by beginning and ending alike and by admitting antithetical comparison from the sense of the passage.

We might write a good deal of prosaic poetry as prose,
unmask it as "just verse," deny the versifier a privilege we ac-
cord the poet to invoke an attitude by typographical convention. Poeticizing poor Goodwin and Gulick reveals the
"poetic" attitude we can bring to the driest stuff if we choose,
but it does not show so fully as it might how even the best

poet, the most practiced reader, depends on typography. Anyone who has tried to read a Greek manuscript written without word or line divisions will know how profoundly disoriented the modern reader feels when bereft of typographical convention.

We may get some idea of this by simply writing out a familiar sonnet in prose. I shall not indent it here, since that itself lends a kind of emphasis. "Margaret, are you grieving over golden grove unleaving? Leaves, like the things of man, you, with your fresh thoughts care for, can you? Ah! As the heart grows older, it will come to such sights colder, by and by, nor spare a sigh, though worlds of wanwood leafmeal lie. And yet you will weep, and know why. Now, no matter, child, the name. Sorrow's springs are the same. Nor mouth had, no, nor mind expressed, what heart heard of, ghost guessed. It is the blight man was born for. It is Margaret you mourn for." I've tinkered with the punctuation a bit and omitted the accent marks Hopkins supplies. What's left is no more "Spring and Fall" than what comes to Southern California.

I wanted this example, like the first, to be extreme. It shows up our attitudes so much better. Hopkins's exquisite sonnet resists prosing as much as any poem can. Yet how it sings in verse:

> Márgarét, are you gríeving
> Over Goldengrove unleaving?
> Leáves, líke the things of man, you
> With your fresh thoughts care for, can you?
> Áh! ás the heart grows older
> It will come to such sights colder
> By and by, nor spare a sigh

Though worlds of wanwood leafmeal lie,
And yet you wíll weep and know why.
Now no matter, child, the name:
Sórrow's spríngs áre the same.
Nor mouth had, no nor mind, expressed
What heart heard of, ghost guessed:
It ís the blight man was born for,
It is Margaret you mourn for.

"Spring and Fall" enforces differences between prose and verse usually considered essential, meter and rhyme. Prose cannot be preponderantly regular in its rhythm, cannot have, though it may occasionally use, meter. Nor can it rhyme with frequency or pattern. The distinction is a clear one, but what good is it? To say that any written utterance which uses meter and rhyme past an arbitrarily decided point must be called poetry, simply makes a quantitative definition impossible to sustain. How many rhymes are allowed in prose? How metrical may it be? We return finally to typography: print it as poetry and it is poetry.

In principle, then, prose uses any rhythm it wants, any rhyme, any pattern of repetition. Prose will not necessarily be bad because it uses these in combination or frequently. It will be another kind of prose, demand another attitude. If it wishes to elicit that attitude explicitly, it will use rhymes frequently, meter obviously. If it wishes to elicit that attitude preponderantly, it may elect to use typography to trigger it. It then becomes poetry. But what was "bad" in prose does not automatically become "good" in verse. Nor the other way around. No essential division separates the two. No one can ever say about any kind of prose, that "this kind of thing would do very well in poetry, but it is not suitable for prose." General rules of this sort are nonsense. Prose can be intrinsically "poetic" in courting the pleasures of language as much as poetry, as much as humankind itself.

Rhythm in prose has long vexed scholars. How rhythmical is this style or that? What effects emerge? How much rhythm ought prose of this sort or that to have? How do you describe the rhythm of a prose text? How recreate it? To these add, And how does anyone learn to feel and see the rhythms in prose? For if prose rhythm has been a problem to scholars, to American students it appears a mystification, terra incognita. It is no mystery why. H. W. Fowler's usual good sense seized the point immediately: "It is an instinct cultivatable by those on whom nature has not bestowed it, but on one condition only—that they will make a practice of reading aloud" (*Modern English Usage,* p. 504). Reading aloud is precisely what no one in America does anymore. To an American university student, the prospect of reading a literary text aloud in class produces a response akin to lockjaw. Reading aloud. An alien activity.

Motives for this paralysis lead us deep into the problem of prose rhythm. Shyness only begins to explain the phenomenon. A reading is a performance. A convincing reader must understand the prose being read. To avoid the monotone haste that swallows prose like castor oil, the voice must vary pitch, something most Americans do not do. Emphasis must be added, tone considered. The reader, that is, must pick a spirit in which to read. She must choose a relationship with the audience. Sentences must be shaped by the intonation. In long passages, a longer rhythm of thought or argument will emerge, as well as the shorter rhythm of individual sentences. Reading aloud renders a style, in our sense of the word, opaque. The stylistic surface must be pondered. The singsong monotone, rhythmical counterpart to the scientific attitude, does not clarify concepts; it obscures them. It does so by boring the reader. A student can be trained to look through a written verbal surface to the concepts lurking beneath. It is much harder to ignore a speaking voice. Try reading one of Hamlet's speeches in a nasal monotone.

Rhetorical performance, of course, was what reading once meant. A Greek or Roman schoolboy did not whiffle through his assignment at a pace inculcated by the Jet-Speed Dynamic Reading Institute. He first studied it intensively. He isolated and remarked the figures of speech. He analyzed the imagery. He studied the shape of a sentence and devised a speech rhythm to elucidate that shape. He selected appropriate gestures for significant junctures. He rehearsed the stages of the argument until the thought moved with a rhythm of its own. Then he memorized the passage, rehearsed it a dozen times. He was then ready to perform it—aloud. Under such a pedagogy, rhythm cannot be a separate study. It grows naturally from the way the prose is addressed. A system of rhythm, for example the series of rhythmic patterns for sentence-closings that the Middle Ages charted, the *clausulae*, was not planned, but simply described what the practice of declamation itself created.

Prose, under such a proceeding, cannot be approached with the scientific attitude alone. Preoccupation with form, with the play attitude, is immediate and continual. A performance is played. The text must be recreated. Some such pedagogy as this is desperately needed in English classes in America today. Students are sometimes asked to memorize a passage of verse. But I have never—Gettysburg Address excepted—heard of a student being asked to memorize and declaim a passage of prose. The debater's training, like Freshman Composition, emphasizes the argument rather than the stylistic surface. This is movement in precisely the wrong direction.

And the speed-reading course is plain lunacy. Its mere premise horrifies: reading is something to be gotten through. Seldom has the American dislike and suspicion of words shown so clearly. Words are to be gotten over with. Mumblespeak *has* to be read this way, of course, but the pattern lingers—you abolish not mumblespeak but humane reading. The ads for such courses always depict a clean-cut young fellow sitting beside a four-foot pile of books, with a caption something like "Bill Herkimer and his Monday's before-breakfast reading." One of the books I noticed in such an ad was *Moby Dick,* and another *Paradise Lost.*

Before prose rhythm can be sensibly considered, one must redefine reading. It cannot be a jet flight coast-to-coast. It must be a slow walk in the country, taken, as all such walks should be, partly for the walking itself. Every course in composition ought to be a course in Slow Reading. To read a prose text aloud, again and again, is the most important single act you can perform, if you are to understand its style. As for rhythm, if you do not read aloud (at least with the mind's ear), there will not be any. Rhythm cannot be studied by itself, directly. Until a text is read aloud there is no rhythm to study. Of course we can silent-read for rhythm, but only if we have learned, paradoxically, how to read aloud silently. Until you have explored this dimension of prose style, you will not know it is there. Once you have explored it, you'll find a passage of mumblespeak literally unreadable. With luck, you may not write any more of it yourself.

To consider rhythm, then, you must hear it. To hear it you must read aloud. To read aloud means bringing the play attitude to prose. Thus, to the degree that a prose has rhythm, it will less welcome the play attitude than demand it. It seems no accident that scientific prose, the neutral style, is usually rhythmless, unemphatic, or cacorhythmic. Be consistent enough about prose's not needing rhythm and it will soon have none. Pick up a newspaper and try to read it—really read it. The prose does not usually welcome such attention.

The scholar's difficulty with prose rhythm arises directly from the situation just described. To hear rhythm you must perform the prose, and no two performances are ever the same. That no two performances of verse are ever the same seldom enters these discussions, such is the zeal displayed to distinguish prose and verse rhythm on the basis of regularity, of meter. So Saintsbury in his exhaustive and exhausting *History of English Prose Rhythm:* "As the essence of verse-metre is its identity (at least in equivalence) and recurrence, so the essence of prose rhythm lies in variety and divergence" (p. 450). And in an earlier encapsulation from the same book: "prose and verse rhythm . . . rhythm diverse and rhythm uniform" (p. 202). W. K. Wimsatt points out the contradiction implicit here by remarking that since "rhythm" implies some kind of regularity, it may not be the best word to use for the patterns of emphasis in prose.

In fact, in talking of prose rhythm, scholars sometimes talk nonsense. So Murry, in *The Problem of Style,* writes of the "flexible, non-insistent rhythm that is proper to prose in the pink of condition," the "lithe glancing movement, swiftly and secretly advancing, which is characteristic of prose" (p. 51). But rhythm is insistence, repetition. What else can it be? Rhythm is promise of pattern. Unless you can see the pattern, acknowledge the promise, how can it exist? What are you trying to measure, or at least point to, when you talk of the "rhythm of prose"? What nomenclature do you use to describe whatever it is you are trying to describe?

Kenneth Burke, in his brilliant discussion of prose style in *Counter-Statement,* employs a vivid analogy for what the reader experiences as prose rhythm:

> The varied rhythms of prose also have their "motor" analogies. A reader sensitive to prose rhythms is like a man hurrying through a crowd; at one time he must halt, at another time he can leap forward; he darts perilously between saunterers; he guards himself in turning sharp corners. We mean that in all rhythmic experiences one's "muscular imagination" is touched. Similarly with sounds, there is some analogy to actual movement, since sounds may rise and fall, and in a remote way one rises and falls with them. (p. 141)

We perform a prose text each time we read it, stretching or squeezing together syllables to gain emphasis. We *clarify* it. We elicit from it a movement of voice by no means implicit in the words considered just as a series of syllables. (You need only read a piece of prose as lifelessly as you can, pronouncing clearly and distinctly and with equal stress upon every syllable in it, to see how much even the worst reading adds to a passage, or perhaps we should say, elicits meaning from it.) Rhythm, to call this complex movement of voice by that name, is thus a cooperative venture, created, like clarity, by reader and writer together. A text may support several rhythms with equal justice; one seldom dominates exclusively. Certain rhythms may be suggested, of course, by syntactical habits or word choices. So Samuel Johnson will force a certain kind of ponderous antitheticality upon us, however we read him. But the rhythm of a passage does not simply exist, as does its imagery: reading has to create it.

So from rhythmical prose arises a natural comparison between rhythm and sense. The sense enters integrally into the performance that creates the rhythm. A writer may choose, or a reader may choose to impose, a rhythm at odds with the sense, thus creating a counterpoint between style and sense. Kingsley Amis has deliciously portrayed such a counterpoint in chapter 22 of *Lucky Jim.* The hero is reading the scholarly paper on which his academic future depends. He is drunk. He has kissed the job good-bye and metamorphosed his performance into one that reflects his real feelings:

> Gradually, but not as gradually as it seemed to some parts of his brain, he began to infuse his tones with a sarcastic, wounding bitterness. Nobody outside a madhouse, he tried to imply, could take seriously a single phrase of this conjectural, nugatory, deluded, tedious rubbish. Within quite a short time he was contriving to sound like an unusually fanatical Nazi trooper in charge of a book-burning reading out to the crowd excerpts from a pamphlet written by a pacifist, Jewish, literate Communist. A growing mutter, half-amused, half-indignant,

arose about him, but he closed his ears to it and read on. Almost unconsciously he began to adopt an unnameable foreign accent and to read faster and faster, his head spinning. . . . He began punctuating his discourse with smothered snorts of derision. He read on, spitting out the syllables like curses, leaving mispronunciations, omissions, spoonerisms uncorrected, turning over the pages of his script like a score-reader following a *presto* movement, raising his voice higher and higher. At last he found his final paragraph confronting him, stopped, and looked at his audience.

The rich pastures of irony lie open to those who "realize" the rhythm of prose (just as a musical performer "realizes" a text when he fills in the harmony a composer has only sketched). Students of meter often refer to the tension between natural word stress and the stress pattern that meter imposes. In prose rhythm an analogous tension waits there for the exploiting. The reader must supply meaning, color it to a degree that poetry seldom permits. Because of this larger freedom, prose is often more fun to read aloud than poetry. Try some and see for yourself.

Afterthoughts

Prose has always had styles, or periods, when it got long-winded (Ciceronian orations and their Renaissance descendents, periodic styles of all kinds) and periods when it buttoned up (Tacitus and his tight-lipped descendents, the scientific styles of the seventeenth century that abjured rhetorical adornment the way the Puritans abjured cosmetics). We're in a buttoned-up stage right now. Bullet points, Power Points, now text messaging (sorry, Txt msg-ing). At either extreme, styles start to play. They both veer off toward poetry. The play element squeezed out by "just the facts, ma'am" bullet points returns via the back door with txt msgs, which so appeal to the adolescent impulse to play. Both impulses are legitimate, and there's no need, as mostly happens, for the long-winded and the buttoned-up to condemn one another.

There is a need, though, for balance. Against txt msgs, I think it might be useful to revive Erasmus's advice in *De Copia* (*Foundations of the Abundant Style*). He pleads for a deliberate training in variation:

> Nature above all delights in variety; in all this huge concourse of things, she has left nothing anywhere unpainted by her wonderful technique of variety. . . . [W]e should frequently take a group of sentences and deliberately set out to express each of them in as many versions as possible. . . . It will be of enormous value to take apart the fabric of poetry and reweave it as prose, and, vice versa, to bind the freer language of prose under the rules of metre, and also to pour the same subject-matter from one form of poetic container into another. (pp. 302–03)

Here's how he does it, constructing variations on the theme of "I much enjoyed receiving your letter":

> At your words a delight of no ordinary kind came over me.
> I was singularly delighted by your epistle. . . .
> To be sure, how your letter delighted my spirits!
> Your brief missive flooded me with inexpressible joy.
> As a result of your letter, I was suffused by an unfamiliar gladness.
> Your communication poured vials of joy on my head.

Your epistle afforded me no small delight.
How delighted I was to read your letter! (pp. 349–50)

And this is only the beginning. His variations continue for four and a half pages.

What on earth is the point of a training like this? It is as far from our present practice as it is possible to be. Yet how else can you explore the immense resources of language, the deep treasury of words from which both prose and poetry are made? Training like this teaches you how to play all the keys on the piano, not just the middle couple of octaves. And when you translate poetry into prose and back again, you learn the difference between the two, or the differences which can distinguish the two, and in ways that no set of definitions will teach you.

Ask yourself a question that I've often wondered about: Why does synonymity develop? It doesn't seem to confer an evolutionary advantage of any sort. This very brief sampling of Erasmus's set of variations suggests one kind of answer. No synonymity is ever exactly synonymous. Each new variation can be read not as an opaque variation on an already determined reality but as a transparent glimpse into a new reality. Thus it is that we imagine new realities and then create them, imagine new selves and then express them. In the ever-changing alternation between condensation and expansion, we should always strive for balance. Since *Style: An Anti-Textbook* first appeared, we've been scrunching up into, now, txt msgs. How about, to restore the balance, roving again in the rich pastures of verbal variation? It is great fun. Try it.

We have moved back to verbal abundance in one way, though, and the movement should encourage us. A friend whose judgment I greatly respected, a scholar of the law and its language, once remarked to me that reading had lost its meaning now that people were "reading" by listening to recorded books in their cars. I couldn't have disagreed more. Prose has regained its voice. Nothing more important has happened for prose since the habit of reading aloud decayed, a habit that lasted at least through Dickensian England.

People are listening to audio books not only in their cars but, via their iPods, while they run, work out at the gym, wherever they take their music. And the eloquent readings that are appearing can reanimate classical works, bring them into the present tense as no amount of scholarly commentary can do. My wife and I started listening to Derek Jacobi's recording of Malory's *Le Morte d'Arthur* while driving to Oregon and we had to stop the disk. The performance was so compelling, so transformative of the fifteenth-century English epic, that I couldn't concentrate on my driving.

I've discussed earlier the growth of a culture of secondary orality. Nothing, not even the cellphone, so well illustrates it as this return to the realm of speech of literature which has for so long dwelt only in the silent land of print. Much of this literature was oral to begin with, meant to be recited, but—and I find this even more exciting—texts, and not all of them literary, that were not conceived for oral performance prove to sound wonderful when read aloud. (As an example, listen to Alexander McCall Smith's *Tears of the Giraffe,* as read by Lisette Lecat. It is available on Apple's iTunes site.) And, if we become used to prose which is read aloud, which is performed, we will have regained that performative practice that both prose and poetry observed in earlier times, when the written text was a score that needed to be performed, not always read silently. When we begin to read aloud silently, when we become aware of what a text would be like if read aloud, we go a long way to restoring voice to our own writing and hearing the voices of other prose styles.

Incidentally, this is the only chapter where I did any major revision. It originally contained a long Winston Churchill passage, which I marked up as a score for reading aloud. The markup was confusing and unsuccessful and so I dropped the attempt to score words on a printed page.

6 Essential Hypocrisies

> The only thing that is indispensable for the possession of a
> good style is personal sincerity.
>
> Sir Herbert Read, *English Prose Style*
>
> Always be sincere, whether you mean it or not.
>
> Flanders and Swann, *At the Drop of a Hat*

A PERSISTENT STRAND of The Books' moralizing has stressed
sincerity in prose composition: don't put on airs; write about
what you have personally experienced; try to develop a style
of your own. Once again, the sum of such counsel is a text
from Polonius. He ends his platitudinous admonitions to his
son Laertes with the famous "To thine own self be true."
What precedes this ringing phrase, unhappily, is more sensible advice on how to fabricate a safe and expedient self to be
true to. Laertes, had he been a bit wittier, could have sensibly
replied, "Self?—what self?" So a student might well reply to
the preaching of The Books, "How can I be sincere when I
haven't yet put together a self to be true to?"

Once again, we surprise an incomplete conception of
prose composition. A self is posited, heart-whole, coherent,
located somewhere halfway between the ears. It exists. The
task is to develop a prose style fully expressive of it. The best
style will most closely imitate the unique configurations of
this unique self. Notice the similarities to the incomplete argument for clarity discussed earlier. Half the process is left
out. Two conceptions of the self have prevailed in the West
from the time of the Greeks onward. One we might call the
"central self," or the soul. To this, the sincerity exhortations

are directed. The second depicts the social, dramatic, role-playing self, people as actors not souls. This dramatic self derives its existence from the society surrounding it. How does one remain true to one's social self? What style expresses the inveterate actor and poseur in all of us? What pedagogy can accommodate this shifting self?

Erik Erikson, in his psychoanalytical version of the Seven Ages of Man argument, sees adolescence as a time of role-experiment. A single self has not yet cohered. In this time of identity crisis, first one role is played, then another. Finally a comfortable dramatic creation falls together into a core self. Around this, the dramatic variations continue to play throughout life. Thus the adolescents speak with literal accuracy of going to college to "find themselves." If Erikson's analysis comes close to the mark, traditional "sincerity" pedagogy should be stood on its head. The adolescent stylist should be encouraged to impersonate other people, not "be himself." He should imitate the historical styles until he can live them with ease. He will then feel, and embody, the historical "selves" they express. Every prose style allegorizes a life style. These life styles will become available to an eclectic effort to build a self of one's own. To ask someone to develop a style before he has a self to start from reveals once again The Books' fondness for basing their pedagogy on a vacuum.

The only real stylistic sincerity an adolescent can grasp is a connoisseur's attitude toward language. This stage of selfhood needs, for prose as for life, an exposure to many styles —the more bizarre and self-conscious the better. Traditional pedagogy clamors for the opposite. It insists on a selection of trendy contemporary essays in a neutral expository prose that filters out self. Or we encounter a version of progressive education's "creativity." Here the student gushes. "Right out of the old guts," as Terry Southern put it, "onto the goddam paper." Both strategies premise a self not yet there. The will for it is immensely strong, however. Erikson anatomizes at length the adolescent desire for "rock bottom," for a central orientation or interpretative point of view, a set of spiritual and intellectual coordinates within which a world can be constructed. What pedagogy is demanded here? How can we fit such strong desire for a central norm into the stylistic eclecticism just described? Clearly, normative prose, invisible clarity, defeats this purpose. It cannot express the self, it evaporates it. If real "sincerity" for the student of style means trying to experiment with social selves to find a central one, how can stylistic instruction help?

Such a search is no longer exclusively adolescent. Adulthood for Western man requires just this self-conscious juggling act to hold together the two concepts of self, social and central. A stylistic diagram representing such a tension would go something like this. No single, normative style is forced on us, just as, unless we are psychotic, no single self is forced on us. We choose. This choice, always to some extent arbitrary, must build on the fullest survey of possible styles. To speak in a figure, circumference becomes center. "Rock bottom" is found by charting boundary conditions for expressive style in one's own language. This range of expressivity has limits, however. Thought can express itself only through style. (Some kind of stylization is inevitable, even if only the stylistic act of renouncing style.) And the devices of style are not unlimited. The expressive range of a language works like a jukebox. It can play a great many tunes but not an unlimited number. Individual combinations will be, for practical purposes, unlimited, but not the constitutive elements. Thus "rock bottom" for stylistic instruction would seem to be a comprehensive survey, as self-conscious as possible, of the basic devices of style available in English. This can be historical or analytical, diachronic or synchronic—it doesn't matter. But it is essential to see that the quest for "sincerity" leads not to an examination of feelings but to an examination of words. Sincerity begins not in feelings but in sentences.

It follows that a central problem of the composition course—what to write about, what to say—is largely irrelevant to the search for sincerity. What to say should be supplied. A range of opinions ought to be furnished and surveyed along with a range of styles. There is, at rock bottom, no call for "originality." It ought not to be forced. If a student hasn't any opinions, let her be given some. Written utterance, after all, strives for imposture. What is writing's built-in advantage if not that, in it, we can pretend to be brighter than we are?

Much has been written about prose that gains authority through the speaking voice. It gains still more by manipulating time scale. We condense ten hours' writing and thinking into one hour's reading. The best ad-libbers always prepare their spontaneity. Writing's advantage, as a presentation of self, is not that it allows us to adopt the mannerisms of speech but that it allows us to adopt the tempo of speech without its hesitant waste.

If writing is organization of thought, it is also, and by the same logic, falsification of thought, imposture. (Thus stream-of-consciousness fictionists, seeking a new style closer to the real tempo of spontaneous thinking, have to fabricate a "random" pattern that ends up making some kind of sense.) Supplying a set of opinions to be presented and developed as forcefully as possible simply brings into self-consciousness the coercion that writing always practices on thought, and hence on us, on our "sincerity." And the self-consciousness frees us, to the extent that we can be freed, from that coercion. If we know what puts limits on our sincerity, what conditions it, we can attain a kind of sincerity beyond the conditioning. Thus, for prose style, the way to sincerity lies through verbal artifice, not around it. Spontaneity, or sincerity, in the composition course, is largely an affair of manner, not matter.

Again, it follows that the object of study should be the stylistic surface. Classical treatises of rhetoric, though they always distinguish the five component parts of oratory, tend to spend a disproportionate amount of their time on one—style—and especially on the "figures," the surface configurations and ornaments of style. Now we can see why. Such a concentration results naturally from the attempt to teach style. Stylistic instruction, therefore, should not try to do away with ornament, it should make love to it. It should attempt to develop a calculus between stylistic and emotional effect. We might instance the pun. The Books deplore it, of course, or allegorize it rather, as an example of language's undependability on the one hand, and its free delights (two meanings from one) on the other.

The study of syntax becomes, in such a calculus, a study in the dynamics of emotional energy. Sincerity will compel us to create, in our sentences' syntax, a model for thc emotion we wish to express. The more flexible and inclusive our syntactical and ornamental repertoire, the more "sincere" our prose can become. To describe the full range of such a repertoire has been tried repeatedly in the past. The emphatic effect of euphony and alliteration, the suspensive effect of participles, the nonlogical identities of rhyme, the verb tenses as forms of awareness—these and a hundred more have been cataloged. What is required now is not to ignore this resource but to see in it the building blocks for sincerity in prose.

As a brief example of this kind of stylistic sincerity, consider the two basic stylistic patterns for prose that have been distinguished since the Greeks. They have been called the running style and the compact or periodic style. Here is a fair example of the running style, from Virginia Woolf's novel *To the Lighthouse:*

> But what after all is one night? A short space, especially when the darkness dims so soon, and so soon a bird sings, a cock crows, or a faint green quickens, like a turning leaf, in the hollow of the wave. Night, however, succeeds to night. The winter holds a pack of them in store and deals them equally, evenly, with indefatigable fingers. They lengthen; they darken. Some of them hold aloft clear planets, plates of brightness. The autumn trees, ravaged as they are, take on the flash of tattered flags kindling in the gloom of cool cathedral caves where gold letters on marble pages describe death in battle and how bones bleach and burn far away in Indian sands. The autumn trees gleam in the yellow moonlight, in the light of harvest moons, the light which mellows the energy of labour, and smooths the stubble, and brings the wave lapping blue to the shore. (p. 192)

Syntax follows sense, either a pattern of association, or of subject, or as here, a chronological sequence. What follows builds upon what went before, modifies it, restates it. A *diachronic* style, we might call it, one that acknowledges the passage of time. It often creates immediacy and action, as in this passage from Henry Fielding's 1741 *Shamela.* Fielding was parodying the adventures of a virtuous servant-girl described in Samuel Richardson's moral fable, *Pamela,* which had appeared to wide acclaim the previous year:

> O Madam, I have strange things to tell you! As I was reading . . . in comes my master—to be sure he is a precious one. Pamela, says he, what book is that? I warrant you Rochester's poems. —No, forsooth, says I, as pertly as I could; why how now saucy chops, boldface, says he—Mighty pretty words, says I, pert again. —Yes (says he) you are a d—d, impudent, stinking, cursed, confounded jade, and I have a great mind to kick your a—. You, kiss—says I. A-gad, says he, and so I will; with that he caught me in his arms, and kissed me till he made my face all over fire. Now this served purely, you know, to put upon the fool for anger. O! What precious fools men are! And so I flung from him in a mighty rage, and pretended as how I would go out at the door; but when I came to the end of the room, I stood still, and my master cried out, hussy, slut, saucebox, boldface, come hither—Yes, to be sure, says I; why don't you come, says he; what should I come for, says I; if you don't come to me, I'll come to you, says he; I shan't come to you, I assure you, says I. Upon which he run up, caught me in his arms, and flung me upon a chair, and began to offer to touch my under-petticoat. Sir, says I, you had better not offer to be rude; well, says he, no more I won't then; and away he went out of the room. I was so mad to be sure I could have cried. (pp. 311–12)

Exaggerated movement, this. Slow it down, and you get this lovely obituary from the nineteenth-century *Greville Memoirs:*

Death, which has been so busy this year, and striking so indiscriminately, took off a person of a very different description on Sunday last. On that day, after a protracted and painful illness, my uncle's widow, Lady William Bentinck, was released from her sufferings. A more amiable and excellent woman never existed in the world. She was overflowing with affections, sympathies, and kindness, not only perfectly unselfish, but with a scrupulous fear, carried to exaggeration, of trespassing upon the ease or convenience of others. Though she had passed all her life in the world, been placed in great situations, and had mingled habitually and familiarly with eminent people, she never was the least elated or spoiled by her prosperity. Her mind was pure, simple, natural, and humble. She was not merely charitable, but was charity itself, not only in relieving and assisting the necessitous, but in always putting the most indulgent constructions on the motives and conduct of others, in a childlike simplicity, in believing the best of everybody, and an incredulity of evil report, which proceeded from a mind itself incapable of doing wrong. . . . Hers was one of those rare dispositions which nature had made of its very best materials. She was gentle and cheerful, and, without being clever, was one of those people whom everybody likes, and whose society was universally agreeable, from a certain undefinable charm of sympathy and benevolence which breathed in her, and which was more potent, attractive, and attaching than great talents or extensive information, to neither of which she had any pretension. (pp. 160–61)

The periodic style works differently. It encloses time into a single, syntactically controllable unit, treats experience synchronically rather than diachronically. Here, arrangement controls, not time. In it, order triumphs; in the running style, order operates. The running style surprises the mind operating; in the periodic style, the mind has finished its work. Here is the Great Periodist himself, Samuel Johnson, concluding his *Life of Milton:*

> The highest praise of genius is original invention. Milton cannot be said to have contrived the structure of an epick poem, and therefore must yield to that vigour and amplitude of mind to which all generations must be indebted for the art of poetical narration, for the texture of the fable, the variation of incidents, the interposition of dialogue, and all the stratagems that surprise and enchain attention. But, of all the borrowers from Homer, Milton is perhaps the least indebted. He was naturally a thinker for himself, confident of his own abilities, and disdainful of help or hindrance: he did not refuse admission to the thoughts or images of his predecessors, but he did not seek them. From his contemporaries he neither courted nor received support; there is in his writings nothing by which the pride of other authors might be gratified, or favour gained; no exchange of praise, nor solicitation of support. His great works were performed under discountenance, and in blindness, but difficulties vanished at his touch; he was born for whatever is arduous; and his work is not the greatest of heroick poems, only because it is not the first. (pp. 841–42)

In this style, boundary conditions for the sentence expand. A great deal is arranged in balanced antithesis, parallel, and contrast, and arranged with utmost clarity. Judgment has been pronounced. Process of mind does not show. This style has its narrative echo on a lower order of periodicity. Here is

the opening paragraph of S. N. Behrman's biography of Lord
Duveen of Millbank:

> When Joseph Duveen, the most spectacular art dealer of all
> time, travelled from one to another of his three galleries, in
> Paris, New York, and London, his business, including a certain
> amount of his stock in trade, travelled with him. His business
> was highly personal, and during his absence his establishments
> dozed. They jumped to attention only upon the kinetic arrival
> of the Master. Early in life, Duveen—who became Lord Duveen
> of Millbank before he died in 1939, at the age of sixty-nine—
> noticed that Europe had plenty of art and America had plenty
> of money, and his entire astonishing career was the product of
> that simple observation. Beginning in 1886, when he was seven-
> teen, he was perpetually journeying between Europe, where he
> stocked up, and America, where he sold. In later years, his an-
> nual itinerary was relatively fixed: At the end of May, he would
> leave New York for London, where he spent June and July; then
> he would go to Paris for a week or two; from there he would
> go to Vittel, a health resort in the Vosges Mountains, where he
> took a three-week cure; from Vittel he would return to Paris for
> another fortnight; after that, he would go back to London; some
> time in September, he would set sail for New York, where he
> stayed through the winter and early spring. (p. 1)

This is the same *kind* of style Johnson uses, but the corners
are softened, habits varied. The word *períodos* in Greek meant
a going-around, a circuit, and thus came to mean a well-
rounded sentence, an extensive survey, and one with shape.
The periodic style, then, may represent pattern, and the running style, process.

A nomenclature has been built on this fundamental division, and subcategories spun off it. But other nomenclatures

could be devised, departing from other antithetical comparisons or tripartite divisions. Grammatical categories could function as a terminology. We might have the simple-sentence style, as illustrated by Hemingway, the compound-complex, as in the later Henry James, or, as with Faulkner, an ever-mutating combination. These categories refer to grammar only; the periodic-running distinction, to sense, syntax, and rhythm. The most common descriptions of styles refer to effect on the reader, a terminology of impression. The mind of the beholder is described, not the style itself: "racy," "flip," "informal." The linguist Charles Bally defined style as the force *parole* exerts on *langue*. (*Langue* is the inherited capability of a language, *parole* the use an individual makes of it, the reality he wrings from potentiality.) Apply this definition of style, and the impressionistic terminology seems a necessity, since the *parole* is a category unto itself, unique, available to description only through the unique particularity of defining metaphor.

A sentence, then, has sound, shape, and significance. Just as there is no canonical formula for the relationship of the three, there is no canonical formula for *describing* the relationship among the three. How many types of prose style are there? Two or more, depending on what categories are selected. I suggested earlier a criterion of self-consciousness. Other reader-writer criteria might develop from this: a relationship of authority, Christ's teaching in the Gospels; a bargaining relationship, the rhetorical contest of the marketplace; a supplication, as in prayer. Descriptive definitions of style are potentially numerous. Which is used—or invoked— seems less important than the stylistic self-consciousness that comes from applying one.

The Books, then, offer a simplistic conception of sincerity in prose because they proceed from a simplistic conception of self. If the central self is established through a pattern of experimentation with social or dramatic selves—with roles—then sincerity in prose will have to follow a similar pattern and find a central style by playing at, and with, a great many styles. And the two processes will influence one another. To play with styles is to play with roles, with ways of thinking and, thus, ways of being. Prose style is always a presentation of self. Its pedagogy, therefore, ought to follow what we know about the formation of self. Style is indeed, as Buffon most famously said, the man himself—but the man sometimes as he is, sometimes as he wants to be, sometimes as he is palpably pretending to be, sometimes, as in comedy, both as he pretends to be and as he is. Stylistic pedagogy ought to cover the whole range. Only by doing so can it perform its authentic social duty: to enhance both clear communication between citizens and the selfhood of the citizens who are communicating.

Afterthoughts

I HAD NO WAY of knowing, when I wrote this chapter, that the greatest opportunity for role-playing in human history was about to open. There seems no limit to the fictional identities people can adopt online, or the pleasure they take in doing so. A very great deal has been written in the intervening years about the nature of the consciously dramatized social self, but none of it can hold a candle to the games of self played on the Internet. Social networking sites like *MySpace* and *Facebook* testify to a hunger for community, we are told. Well, yes, but what they really demonstrate is a hunger for formalized role-playing, what the advertising people are now calling "personal brands." *YouTube* invites you to "broadcast yourself" through your own videos. This explosion of trial identities in multimedia expression shows how strongly we want to try out alternate selves, especially in adolescence, and how great a role such rehearsals play in finally nailing down a central self. And it enforces the point of this chapter: how incomplete and unsatisfying the "sincerity" standard proves for prose. In this new world of trial identities, why not use prose styles, too, to find your space—or spaces? That, at least, was what I argued for in this chapter.

I prefaced the chapter with two epigraphs about sincerity, Sir Herbert Read's earnest exhortation and Flanders and Swann's ironic one. I suggested that we might think of "sincerity" in prose as emerging from basic prose styles, something more in line with Flanders and Swann than Sir Herbert Read, and I gave some examples. I meant them to illustrate that "sincerity" has a formal, as well as an emotional, element and that this formal element provides the necessary substrate for style as personality. In hindsight, I'm not sure I succeeded in this. See what you think. I dealt with the basic prose styles in a later book (*Analyzing Prose*) and made the point more clearly there.

I think, however, that from all the online role-playing experiments will emerge a set of basic templates for forming a "personal brand" in much the same way the basic templates for prose style help us in finding the styles that suit us best. It will be interesting to see if this works out to be true. Meanwhile, the similarity between the pedagogy of role-playing experiment which I advocate for prose style in this chapter and the kind of role-playing experiment currently thriving all around us remains striking. It suggests that a pedagogy using prose style exercises in this way would fit easily into the current scene.

7 The Ultimate Morality of Mind

> The style is the man. Rather say the style is the way the man
> takes himself. . . . If it is with outer seriousness, it must be
> with inner humor. If it is with outer humor, it must be with
> inner seriousness.
>
> Robert Frost, *Letters*

As PHILOSOPHIC COUNTERPART to the American pedagogy
of clarity, a very high seriousness toward the cultural role of
language has emerged. Every prophet of doom, when chronicling our national descent down the rat hole of his choice,
deplores the current state of our language. So Jacques Barzun, in his brilliant and witty *The House of Intellect,* warns us
that "The state of the mother tongue is in fact the index of
our control over destiny." And the current state is, of course,
grotesque. Barzun poses the problem fairly. Language reveals
national psychoses but does not necessarily cause them.

Most have not been so cautious. For them, language is
usually the cause, the villain. Solve the prose problem—If
Everyone Would Only Be Clear—and the rest will fade away.
In as much as this varies St. Thomas More's "All things will
not be well until all men are good—Which I do not think
will be Lo! these many long years," no one can quarrel with
it. Any causal connection more particular than this has never
been proven. Prophets who wish people would be clearer
really wish, like Barzun, that they would be a little brighter.
Again, no one can quarrel with this.

But the proposition that we are worse off than earlier
times or other countries abides no proof. We cannot go back

and test or control enough variables. And of course—the problem of infinite regress—we have to use language to talk about language. The whole question, put in these terms, becomes futile. We are, as I said earlier, the only country ever prosperous and democratic enough to *have* a prose problem. This book has argued that we need a new theory and pedagogy of prose style to meet a new problem. The old crackpot utilitarianism won't work. If changes in language or language instruction can change the fate of nations, we're the first country in a position to do anything about it. There are, then, two questions. Does instruction in language make any difference for our future? And is that linguistic future really so desperate as it seems? The preceding chapters have suggested answers to the first question. Before reviewing them, let me put the case for desperation as strongly as possible and then see what can be said against it.

The case for desperation: Failure to pay the costs of mass education has given the schools chronic intellectual heart trouble for most of this century, and the universities now follow suit. Few care to write well and fewer know how. The media bombardment converts us into, if not McLuhan's global village, at least something unexpected. Our national conversation resembles a chatterbox convention where everyone says "You know?" and nobody knows, like. Our political utterance is congested with what my research assistant, in an inspired typographical error, rendered as "Eisenhoweverese." Our sentimental mass democracy denies the very idea of standards. Everybody just lets it all hang out. We reduce ourselves to machines with an electronic slang of "plugged-in" and "turned-on." The New Left, like the Neo Right, addicts itself to tantrum prose. We are suffering from a ludicrous case of national euphemism.

Atop all this, twirling its dark moustache, sits the real villain, advertising. Here are two truly wise men on the subject. First, Northrop Frye:

> The mob's version of high style is advertising, the verbal art of penetrating the mind by prodding the reflexes of the ego. As long as society retains any freedom, such advertising may be largely harmless, because everybody knows that it is only a kind of ironic game. As soon as society loses its freedom, mob high style is taken over by the new masters, to become what is usually called propaganda. Then, of course, the moral effects become much more pernicious. Both advertising and propaganda, however, represent the conscious or unconscious pressure on a genuine society to force it into a mass society, which can only be done by debasing the arts. (*The Well-Tempered Critic,* p. 46)

We're flooded, then, with mob style. In *Democracy and the Student Left,* George F. Kennan ranks it as a danger just behind war and pollution:

> Next to it [ecology] I would have to put something that will surprise most people—something that many people, in fact, will fail utterly to understand. This is the phenomenon of American advertising, and the extent to which it has been permitted to dominate and exploit the entire process of public communication in our country. It is to me positively inconceivable that the whole great, infinitely responsible function of mass communication, including very important phases of the educational process, should be farmed out—as something

to be mined for whatever profit there may be in it—to people whose function and responsibility have nothing to do with the truth—whose function and responsibility, in fact, are concerned with the peddling of what is, by definition, untruth, and the peddling of it in trivial, inane forms that are positively debauching in their effect on the human understanding. After the heedless destruction of natural environment, I regard this —not advertising as such, but the consignment to the advertiser of the entire mass communications process, as a concession to be exploited by it for commercial gain—as probably the greatest evil of our national life. We will not, I think, have a healthy intellectual climate in this country, a successful system of education, a sound press, or a proper vitality of artistic and recreational life, until advertising is rigorously separated from every form of legitimate cultural and intellectual communication—until advertisements are removed from every printed page containing material that has claim to intellectual or artistic integrity and from every television or radio program that has these same pretensions, from every roadside and every bit of countryside that purports to offer to the traveler a glimpse of what his continent once was and once might be. (pp. 230–32)

The media, the only agency that can educate in a mass society, have been whored out for profit. The power that should educate the imagination instead brutalizes it. The media, advertising especially, cultivate inattention as a habit, an ingrained pattern of reading and seeing. Though it holds repetition a premise, the ad is a one-time experience. Advertising repels wonder. It degrades willing suspension of disbelief into perpetual cynical suspicion. Advertising uses up language; a thousand novels could not wear it out so fast. Advertising pollutes language.

The palpable falsity of advertising continually reinforces a view of language as the father of lies. Daniel Boorstin has written eloquently on the falsity of American life, its dominant pseudo quality, in *The Image: A Guide to Pseudo-Events in America.* Advertising language is pseudo language, creating the substance it pretends to describe. One recent widely publicized study showed that even three- and four-year-old children had developed a full-fledged suspicion of ads, and hence of language. A kind of depraved poetry, it invents an "image" which, unlike the products bought in its name, retreats before us like a mirage.

End of case for desperation. It's a powerful one. But is it fair to how we stand now? Doesn't it ignore the enormous hunger for style and stylistic play now abroad in America? This urge to stylize overwhelms anyone who walks around an American campus. Wild eclecticism of dress, public love-making, consciously exaggerated addiction to slang, robust bearding of the bourgeois—all testify to a hunger for style. Even the widespread dissatisfaction with the quality of instruction may stem from the styleless democracy of prevailing student-professor relationships. The whole university scene, as the *institution* creates it, apotheosizes drab, offers the student no opportunity to play the student formally.

Hunger for style may explain the contribution that black Americans are making to the American campus. Rich in style, their slang now seems destined to capture the straight culture as it captured the hippie one. Raw, brutal, intensely metaphorical, it feeds the hungers that scientific prose starves. Since nobody has trained them in the scientific attitude, black Americans have never lost the sense of play with words.

We find around us, then, both intense stylization (and its superficial symptom, faddishness) and intense hunger for style—especially for style in behavior, for drama. (Much of the sit-in phenomenon can be traced to students' hunger to dramatize their roles as students, to dramatize feelings balked of public manifestation.) To feel fully, you must feel publicly. You must stylize your feelings. Thus happenings and participatory theater. It is even possible to subsume one of the most unsavory of the recent campus phenomena, the Free and Filthy Speech movements, under the rubric of stylistic hunger. Foul language seems to satisfy a degraded hunger for sacramental speech, for a language at its least transparent and utilitarian.

We might even find in the full sacramental speech of America—advertising—signs of the play spirit. The crosstalk between ads (VW, Hertz, Avis), the frequent punning and verbal play, the TV commercials grown into minidramas that appeal, increasingly, through style. Dishonest though it be, might not advertising depart from premises more honest than those marshaled by the pedagogy of clarity and closer to the real nature of human motive? Advertising causes people to mistrust language, but might it not also be teaching people to enjoy it? The picture of the young child singing an ad cliché to herself fills us with loathing. We'd prefer her to be rehearsing "Shall I compare thee to a summer's day."

But isn't the enjoyment of language rather like reading? It's a habit. What difference if it's trash that gets you in the habit? Language in advertising is at least always visible. It is not argued out of existence. And it is full of affect, of feeling, of desire. Feeling and color. Opaque. If it is the poetry of the poor—and in the life of the imagination most of America is poor—it is certainly bad poetry. But isn't this better than none? Nothing is what it replaces. If the state of our mother tongue can be sustained and embellished only by a people self-conscious about language, advertising may do more to engender this self-consciousness than the transparent, denotative prose that ignores language to concentrate exclusively on meaning.

A few other signs hint that we are becoming self-conscious, or style-conscious, about our language. The most obvious looms so large we tend to ignore it—the composition crisis itself. We may meet it with the wrong strategy, but that we want to meet it at all argues a high level of awareness. We're plagued by jargon, but as we've seen, people now counter by playing with it. Black American idiom is played at by the stylistically deprived upper-middle class. The minorities have developed a proud self-consciousness about their own languages and speak them symbolically. Even the Webster's Third outcry—too many colloquialisms accepted as standard—may fit here. People were upset because The Great Game of Correct Usage seemed about to fold its tents. Needless fear—a game so pleasant as correctness will be reinvented spontaneously.

Such stylistic self-consciousness makes sense. American society as a whole is going this way. Increasingly self-conscious about economy, ethics, structure of self, why should we not be about language? A mass society now reenacts the aristocratic Renaissance discovery that man's nature is artifice. Our present concern with pseudo event and our craving for spontaneity testify to a wide shouldering of the Renaissance burden. De Tocqueville predicted—truly as usual—that American writing would ignore niceties of style and decorum, aristocratic elegance. Don't the signs now suggest an aristocratic stage beyond the utilitarian one? We certainly possess the only begetter of aristocratic taste, moneyed leisure. In the future that Alvin Toffler has conjured up in *Future Shock,* utilitarian pressure will evaporate entirely. We won't *have* to do anything. Everything will be done for pleasure. The proud slogans of the Renaissance will become literally true. Man will remake himself in whatever form or style he chooses. We shall have to develop both acute self-consciousness and an equally acute sense of style. Electronic intelligence may entirely appropriate prose's obligation to communicate concepts. Such a world speaks and writes entirely for pleasure, entirely for style. The Books' ideal stylist may find himself endowed, in de Maupassant's phrase, "with a perspicacity which strongly resembles incompetence."

The squirrel chatter present, then, does not lack signs of hope. We may come to think of our verbal environment as we are learning to think of our physical environment, as something to be cultivated and cherished, not taken for granted. Assuming this to be so, what benefits might accrue? Beyond its self-liquidating help in communicating concept, is prose style good for anything?

We've rehearsed some answers already. A style can serve as paradigm for a social role, an identity. Modern personality theory suggests that we all have many personalities, many selves among whom we choose as occasion requires. Many styles, many selves—which style is which man? Buffon's maxim proves more serviceable when inverted. The man? He is the style itself. A good style can *create* a personality. When he finds it does so consistently, the writer will name it, as Samuel Clemens named Mark Twain. Flaubert called style "une manière de voir," a way of seeing. We might call it a way of behaving. We have arrived at life style, the shape we give our lives.

A style, thought of in this way, might seem much like a psychological experiment—a set of boundary conditions within which meaningful answers can be found. Our language sets limits to what we can know and feel. Speak a different language, inhabit a different universe. Style might be viewed as imposing, on a smaller scale, limits to what we can know and how we can feel. On a yet smaller scale, a literary style sets limits to our expectations, to what kinds of experience we look forward to. It creates a closed universe of discourse.

Stylistic awareness, then, makes possible dialogue with ourselves. It may serve the community as much by enriching the communicator as by clarifying the communication. As clearly, it will empower us to enter into the past, look through lost eyes, participate in the past's ways of seeing and thus enrich our own. The study of prose styles serves to introduce, too, a keen self-consciousness about human perception and knowledge. It thus fits neatly into what Daniel Bell and others have seen as the informing principle of the new undergraduate university curriculum—the study of method. Style as visible, self-conscious, opaque, forms part of a curriculum whose center will be self-consciousness, whose rock bottom is an awareness of boundary conditions. The worship of clarity, like the Newtonian concept of matter and the nineteenth-century historian's concept of fact, becomes part of a larger pattern of larger truth. The stylistic spectrum discussed in chapter 3 thus makes sense in terms of, indeed emerges from, a new and promising conception of the undergraduate curriculum.

"In its simplest manifestation," Kenneth Burke maintains, "style is ingratiation" (*Permanence and Change,* p. 50). This leads us down the road opposite from Buffon, from the individual toward society. By a sense of style we socialize ourselves. Style finally becomes, as Burke works it out, social custom:

> Style is a constant meeting of obligations, a state-of-being-without-offense, a repeated doing of the "right" thing. It molds our actions by contingencies, but these contingencies go to the farthest reaches of the communicative. For style (custom) is a complex scheme of what-goes-with-what, carried through all the subtleties of manner and attitudes. Its ample practice in social relationships can take the place of competitive success because it *is* success. (p. 269, n. 2)

Style defines situations, tells us how to act in them. A prose style defines a literary situation. We return to our emphasis on the self-consciousness shared by writer and reader. In society, it is called manners; in literature, decorum. Style as personality implies an agonistic relationship, a contest. We must feel the force of this great man or woman, like it or not. By style as by presence, we are to be overpowered. But style as ingratiation offers an alternative to competition. It aims at the gentlest kind of persuasion, the attempt to make oneself over in the form most agreeable to the other.

The study of prose style reveals its most immediate social applicability viewed under such a definition. For literary decorum can function—probably does, used in this way or not—as a model for social decorum. Value judgments, under such a definition, cannot be absolute. If you say, style being ingratiation, that a style has value independent of its audience, you really posit a certain kind of audience as correct. You are, in effect, making a statement about the trainability of a certain kind of audience. Style, in such a definition, is an orchestration of probable acceptances. If they don't work, it's a bad style.

We move easily from style as ingratiation to A. N. Whitehead's drumroll in *The Aims of Education,* "Style is the ultimate morality of mind" (p. 19). We might argue that the underpinning of morality, the feeling for right behavior, is as much aesthetic as moral judgment. Prose style exercises, and can exorcise too, our range of possible behavior. By allowing the luxury of imaginative rehearsal, it confers real ethical choice, and to this extent frees us from necessity. Ethics at this point touches taste, indeed becomes it.

The study of style constitutes for man an intrinsically satirical, a fundamentally comic pursuit. A style, as Schopenhauer said, is a mask. Stylistic study, by the logic of its address, unmasks us. It teaches us that there is nothing inevitable about our self, or selves, our thoughts, or the words they are clothed in. It demonstrates how much thought sometimes owes to style and, sometimes, how little. It recapitulates the whole range of human dependence on words. Above all, the study of verbal style is radically reductive of motive. It satirizes high seriousness. The art of translation that any teacher performs when she corrects a paper is essentially satirical. She is ridiculing pretense, revealing a simplified and usually demeaning reality behind it. This satire a student must learn to perpetrate on his own prose and his own self. Both yield the same comic awareness of self and the limitations of self. And such comic self-awareness is, of course, the central requirement for the citizen of a self-conscious society. To know that we are mistaken, and necessarily so, is the art of spiritual openness and welcome that makes such a society possible.

Above all, what we learn about ourselves from study of the whole stylistic spectrum is the inevitable self-pleasing ingredient in all human behavior. When we have restricted clarity, the desire to speak plainly, to its proper small segment of the spectrum, we soon come to know that, in the broad range that is left, we entertain concepts because concepts entertain us. Such awareness does not rule out altruistic motive, but it does prevent flattering overestimations. Just as Hamlet discovers that the deepest motive for his own behavior is not revenge but acting the revenge hero, the pleasures of acting for its own sake, so we learn that beneath all our pleas for clarity and expressivity runs a substratum of verbal play.

Motive has always been the question of questions for Freshman Composition. Perhaps more success might flow from assuming, paradoxically, that the deepest motive for writing is not communication at all but the pleasures of writing for its own sake. Writing to others is a writing for ourselves. Clarity in communication may be less the cause of our pleasure in prose than the result.

Afterthoughts

I've argued in a recent book, *The Economics of Attention: Style and Substance in the Age of Information,* that, in our present economy, style and substance change places. The argument goes this way: Economics studies the allocation of scarce commodities. We live, all seem to agree, in a society where information constitutes the real, the fundamental wealth. But information is not scarce; we're drowning in it. What is scarce is the human attention needed to make sense of it. When you ask how attention is allocated in human life, you come to see that style plays a fundamental role in this allocation. In an economy based on physical stuff, style has always been seen to play a secondary role. The primary stuff is the rock you kick with your foot, mine from the ground, form into material well-being. But if the primary stuff is now information, then style—how this information is communicated to us, the packages it comes in—becomes centrally important.

In this chapter, I found with some surprise when I reread it, I was finding my way to this argument. I can't rehearse the winding path here, but readers interested in it might find the first chapter of *The Economics of Attention* (it's titled "Stuff and Fluff") an interesting amplification of the argument I sketch out here.

Advertising plays an ever greater role in an economics of attention, so the issue of its influence is still with us. It was not advertising per se that annoyed Frye and Kennan, I would guess, but the marketplace that advertising represented. Intellectuals have always had a troubled relationship with the marketplace, one which the economist George Stigler examined in a famous essay, "The Intellectual and the Marketplace." I've persisted in stressing the stylistic play that advertising has always embodied, and the playfulness has grown stronger in the last few years, especially in TV advertising. The current game is to tell a very short detective story in which the product being advertised comes as the explanation of the mystery. Try turning the sound off during one of these commercials and you'll see what I mean. Certainly TV advertising has used kinetic text (text that moves and changes shape as it appears on the screen) in ways far more imaginative than the rest of multimedia utterance.

The boat I really missed in thinking about advertising, though, was the way it had become, by the time I wrote the book, the central subject of Pop Art, and hence of art criticism. Pop Art built a revolution around looking *at* advertising rather than, as Frye and Kennan do, *through* it. I tried to make up for this oversight in two subsequent books, *The Electronic Word* and *The Economics of Attention.*

I mentioned de Tocqueville's prediction that American writing would ignore the niceties of style and decorum, aristocratic elegance. I then observed: "Don't the signs now suggest an aristocratic stage beyond the utilitarian one? We certainly possess the only begetter of aristocratic taste, moneyed leisure." My observation has proved true, but about the wrong aspect of American society. Our writing stands as far from aristocratic elegance as ever, but the sophistication of our awareness of design across the visual spectrum, from houses to clothes, has certainly intensified. Design now occupies a far more important role in American life than it did when I wrote. We really are recovering—for better and worse —the Renaissance's stylistic self-consciousness. Pity it hasn't included writing and speaking.

About what we might call "private speaking" I must confess a profound depression. I said in this chapter that "the spastic present . . . does not lack signs of hope." I'm not sure I would say this now. The student conversation I overhear as I walk across campus is dominated by the "like" habit to a degree that must madden any person sensitive to language. "So, I go, like, and he goes, like" and so it goes, like, in the same compulsive pattern devoid of anything that might be called cultivated speech or, even, sense. It was bad enough when I first wrote, but it is much worse now. To take such a "prescriptive attitude," as the linguists call it, is to confess oneself—our worst term of opprobrium—elitist. We find ourselves, here, in the world of "correctness" and all the corrections of correctness that a changed society has brought with it: usage as class-based, nonstandard English as having its own grammar and syntax, dialect as a variation to be cherished, not banished, usage as continually shifting and subject to intense personal prejudice.

Yet a discouraging permanent truth lurks beneath all such debates. As Northrop Frye says in *The Well-Tempered Critic,* "Good writing must be based on good speech; it will never come alive if it is based on reading alone" (p. 34). So what will become of writing when students don't even read much, and when their speech is a witless lurch from "I go" to "she goes" and back?

Debates about usage can easily get silly and often do. Yet, as David Crystal, himself a distinguished linguist, has argued, "Prescriptive attitudes play an important part in defining the educatedness of a society, and should not be glibly dismissed" (*The Cambridge Encyclopedia of the English Language,* p. 367). Especially is this so with students. They need to know what the rules are, indeed that there are such things as rules, before they are encouraged to break them. I would argue, rebarbative as it may seem to modern pedagogy, that traditional English grammar constitutes a useful study that might well be revived.

Something besides fashion or class prejudice is at issue in the "like" habit and the profound inattentiveness to language that it reveals. The prince of prescriptive grammarians and usage experts, H. W. Fowler, put his finger on the issue in a comment in *The King's English.* Just to sketch the context of Fowler's remark is to mark how far from his world spins the world we dwell in. He is talking about the use of the word *individual,* and reminding us that it is not synonymous with "person," and he takes two pages of instance and explanation to do so. Here is how he begins:

> To use *individual* wrongly in the twentieth century stamps a writer, more definitely than almost any other single solecism, not as being generally ignorant or foolish, but as being without the literary sense. . . . Every one who is interested in style at all—which includes every one who aspires to be readable— must at least be aware that there is some mystery about the word, even if he has not penetrated it. (pp. 62–63)

Thus, truly, speaks the clerk of a forgotten mood. Who now pays attention to the mystery of words, much less to a word like *individual*? To do so seems to us a ridiculous affectation. Yet he has isolated the vital quality—"the literary sense"—in any stylistic decision. It is this literary sense that is so utterly lacking in the world of "like." I do not speak here merely of an acquaintance with literature, great or trivial, for it is possible to read either without a "literary sense," an attention to the meaning of individual words and how they live on the stylistic surface. Attend to words in this way and you begin to attend to how you write them and how you speak them. You begin to develop a stylistic self-consciousness. It is a skill which, like riding a bicycle, once learned is never forgotten. And the similarity with riding a bicycle is not superficial. A sensitivity to words gets under your skin; it becomes part of the balance with which you wheel through the world.

It is a great pity that the place where, if anywhere, such skill ought to be imparted—the English Department—has chosen to ignore it. The historical study of the English language must start in the classical languages, Greek and Latin, which preceded it and contributed so strongly to it. A background in these languages no longer forms part of even the ideal package of study. So, too, with the other great source, the Romance languages. In my department, even the root inquiry, a course in the history of the English language, is no longer demanded of doctoral candidates; undergraduate study of the subject is unheard of. Nor is there a course, of course, in prose style.

"Well," you might ask about these nostalgic regrets, "so what?" Does such a "literary sense" about words make any difference in the world of affairs? Turns out, it does. I quoted earlier (pp. 32–33) a *Wall Street Journal* article, published in January 2006, on the ranking of business schools by those who recruit M.B.A.s from them. The attribute that ranked highest for recruiters? "Communications and interpersonal skills." Speaking and writing that lead to the "style that is ingratiation," to a talent for getting along with people. The need for this package of talents comes up, and usually ranks first, in the wish list that the world of affairs perennially presents to the groves of academe. A road really does lead from "the literary sense" to the ordinary uses of ordinary life, and it is this road that *Style: An Anti-Textbook* sought to map.

Sequels

Confession Time

SEVERAL YEARS AFTER I wrote this book, I started a writing program and became a composition administrator! The UCLA Writing Programs was a campus-wide effort, unusual at the time, with courses in many different fields, but it was not a doctrinaire one. The thirty faculty members teaching in it did not follow my own advice in *Style: An Anti-Textbook;* they were free to teach in their own ways and successfully did so. Wasn't I, then, imitating the world I had been satirizing?

Worse still, I wrote a book called *Revising Prose,* which aimed, through a set of rules called the "Paramedic Method," to make the kind of prose my students were writing clearer, briefer (I set a goal of 50% briefer), and, if not more sincere, at least more natural in its voice. The book soon proved a useful guide for writers in many different areas of endeavor, and in its successor editions has remained so.

"No Fair!" my friends (and some less friendly voices) cried. "Look here, Lanham, you can't work both sides of the street." So let me, after all these years, try to explain this inconsistent behavior.

The UCLA Writing Programs first. The faculty faced new tasks, creating writing curricula across the campus. A commonplace now but not then. Who knew what the best way was to do this? The best way seemed, to me at least, to hire some very bright people and turn them loose to be bright about their new tasks in their own ways. And to let them, as far as possible, choose these tasks among the many we had to perform. The result would be, if it worked, a sensitivity to style, both in prose and in curricula and teaching techniques, that would flow from the wisdom of the group rather than being imposed from the top down. No central dogma; no central textbook.

It worked. People rethought, in their own terms, how they taught writing, and from it different kinds of courses and, yes, different textbooks, emerged. So I don't think the administrative structure contradicted the arguments I put forward in the *Anti-Textbook*. It seemed, indeed, the only way to fulfill them.

But what about *Revising Prose*? The book emerged from the student writing I spent so much time reading. Almost all of it seemed to be formulaic, to follow a particular pattern, and this pattern was bureaucratic language, clotted with passives and Latinate euphemism. I christened it "The Official Style"; and the more bureaucratic our world has become the more it has thrived. Since it was a formulaic prose, I offered a formulaic way to revise it. This proved to be a great virtue. It got the writer's nose right down into the verbal surface. This was what I kept arguing for in the *Anti-Textbook*—stylistic analysis. Analysis of a particular style, to be sure, but one that recreated the stylistic awareness that came with the territory in classical rhetorical training. But the argument needed to be broadened; it needed to include the whole range of prose styles. So I wrote another book which did this, *Analyzing Prose*. I started with a particular problem and then pulled the camera back to survey the whole landscape. The two books, taken together, seemed to me a continuation of the argument advanced in this book, not a contradiction of it. All three books are part of the same process and pedagogy —stylistic awareness.

The classical way to teach the arts of public expression, oral and written, involved a continual oscillation from looking at the verbal surface to analyzing how it created meaning. One moved from style to argument and back. It was like breathing in and breathing out. The final aim—as in *Style: An Anti-Textbook* and the books that emerged from it—was respiration.

Sister Miriam in 3D

THE BIGGEST NEWS STORY since this book was written, for our purposes at least, has been the emergence of a new expressive space, the digital electronic space of a computer screen. The frame of this space has been shrinking lately, from desktop computer to laptop, and from laptop to cellphone and iPod, but the principles of expression have remained the same. Words are no longer fixed in print, but move around, can change shape and color, and can be replicated and transmitted almost instantaneously and almost cost-free. Print has always, from the earliest days of woodcuts, been sometimes accompanied by images, but the dominant signal has been words, words in black and white, with no moving distractions to break the reading spell. Now this monopoly of attention has been broken and words must compete with the images and sounds which populate multi-media expression.

This competition has been unwelcome to the world of words, as competition always is to monopolists. We have come, the prophets tell us, to the end of Western culture. Words have fallen victim to cartoons. And there is plenty of evidence to support this view. One of my English department colleagues has noticed that her students misunderstand the literary texts they are asked to read because they do not know the meaning of many common, ordinary English words. Many English teachers have remarked that students simply cannot read ordinary literary texts: they are too complicated. Students read remarkably little outside the assignments they are forced to read. To cope with this incapacity and incompetence, textbooks and newspapers are being "dumbed down." I have already commented on the current speech habits of ordinary conversation.

True it is that cries of outrage at the current low levels of literacy have been with us for a long time. But the skies may really be falling this time, and if so, multimedia expression is part of the reason. For the sake of balance, though, let me present a possible counterstatement to this persuasive pessimism.

In the first place, reading does not seem to be fading from the scene. Our problem is not that too few books are being published but too many; not that too few magazines appear but that the newsstands overflow with them. Words have not retreated from multimedia expression under the pressures of omnipresent imagery and sound; they multiply with each hypertextual link. And more and more of the printed corpus of cultural wisdom is being digitized and made available online. Writing overflows in emails and blogs and people spend a great deal of time reading these pyroclastic flows of words. The binding may be electronic but the text is conventionally print-bound.

But I want to suggest a second reason for interest, at least, and perhaps for optimism as well. Electronic expression has not destroyed traditional Western cultural notation; it has revived it. Manuscript notation has always had a basic visual element because the scribal modes of writing imparted it. The aim of type design has always been transparency, but manuscripts always moved the other way, toward individuation. Sometimes, of course, this scribal variation altered the text, to the great discontentation of textual scholars. But there was often, if not always, a visual beauty in the way the letters were formed, abbreviated, and linked to one another. And, as the tradition of illuminated manuscripts so dramatically shows, the manuscript reader wanted as powerful an imagistic signal as was feasible and affordable. The letters themselves often had a habit of turning into apotropaic animal figures and grotesques. Nor was sound lacking. Reading in the manuscript world mostly meant reading aloud, performing in a social situation. The system of cultural notation before the invention of print mixed its media as well as it knew how. We may deplore the current digital version of this mixture, but we cannot accuse it of lacking respect for its forebears. It is imitating them.

The digital mixture suggests all kinds of new pedagogies for teaching writing, or rather for teaching the expression of which writing now forms only one part. Here is not the place to discuss such possibilities; that would require a book unto itself. But words will continue to form a prominent part of the education in expression.

In the "Origins" foreword to this new edition of the *Anti-Textbook,* I referred to Sister Miriam Joseph's *Shakespeare's Use of the Arts of Language* as a source of inspiration. Let me return to it briefly now. The repertoire of rhetorical figures, of verbal patterns, that she describes was developed by Greek rhetoric as Greece moved from an oral culture, based on a memorized poetic cultural record, to a written culture. How translate the gestures, the habits of voice, the patterns of expression characteristic of speech into their written equivalents? Sister Miriam's compendium represents the results of such an effort, a movement from three-dimensional dynamic space to fixed two-dimensional print. Now we are moving back the other way. Words exist in a three-dimensional dynamic space in some ways very like the oral environment whence they came. What will happen when digital expression allows us to express again these spatial clues? It will be fun to see.

The New Conversation

WE FIND OURSELVES with a new kind of writing, one in which, in its swift interchange between writers, resembles the pace of speech more than writing. One which, with all the fictional personalities that we can assume, seems more like participatory and improvisational fiction than the conversation of daily life. Social networking sites like *MySpace, Facebook,* and *YouTube* create a self-consciousness about our daily identity, which in the past has always led to an equal self-consciousness about verbal expression. Maybe it will for us, but for now it seems to be working in the opposite direction. But there is so much self-conscious discussion about "media" today, and so many ways in which ordinary people can express themselves in these media, that maybe words will take their place in a new environment that people enter for fun.

There certainly are plenty of ways in which verbal self-consciousness can be taught in this new conversation, if we are willing to explore them. If to these new ways we add the old ones, the ones from the world of *Style: An Anti-Textbook*—literature, read and spoken; daily conversation and training therein; public speaking; formal debate training; training in professional languages of all sorts; old-fashioned grammatical and syntactical error-finding; historical study of style; translation from style to style; study of foreign languages; word games; practice in concision and expansion; Erasmus's games in *De Copia*, which develop the ability to say the same thing in many different ways; study of regional dialects and practice in speaking them—if we add all these in, perhaps prose composition teaching and learning will finally emerge from the penalty box. If so, we will be able to see what has always emerged from Shakespeare and Dickens and Emerson and Lincoln: pleasure in words for their own sake and for what they can do to expand the imaginative reality of human beings.

Notes for Further Reading

DAVID CRYSTAL's *The Cambridge Encyclopedia of the English Language* (Cambridge University Press, 1995) provides a history of the language, a discussion of its grammar, vocabulary, and ever-changing usages. Don't be put off by the "encyclopedia" title. It is a wonderful book, clever, witty, learned, and full of neat illustrations and sidebars.

If you need to review traditional English grammar, Michael Strumpf and Auriel Douglas have written a straightforward guide, *The Grammar Bible* (Henry Holt, 2004). Karen Elizabeth Gordon has written a more light-hearted illustrated introduction, *The Deluxe Transitive Vampire: The Ultimate Handbook of Grammar for the Innocent, the Eager, and the Doomed* (Pantheon Books, 1993). I will also have to confess a continuing fondness for a traditional, prescriptive, elitist, English—as against American—grammar, H. W. Fowler and F. G. Fowler's *The King's English* (Oxford University Press, 1931). If you want to step back and take a historical and theoretical view of grammar's place in the scheme of things, Sister Miriam Joseph's *The Trivium: The Liberal Arts of Logic, Grammar, and Rhetoric,* ed. Marguerite McGlinn (Paul Dry Books, 2002) is the place to begin.

For those wishing to read up on punctuation, M. B. Parkes's scholarly and illuminating (and cleverly titled!) survey, *Pause and Effect: Punctuation in the West* (University of California Press, 1993), provides the best general introduction to the subject. Karen Elizabeth Gordon has revised her well-received *The Well-Tempered Sentence* (Ticknor & Fields, 1983) into *The New Well-Tempered Sentence: A Punctuation Handbook for the Innocent, the Eager, and the Doomed* (Pantheon Books, 1993). And if you doubted that a book on punctuation could prove to be a bestseller, Lynne Truss's *Eats, Shoots and Leaves: The Zero Tolerance Approach to Punctuation* (Profile Books, 2003) has proved you wrong.

Several good histories of composition instruction have appeared since the first edition of this book. James J. Murphy has edited *A Short History of Writing Instruction: From Ancient Greece to Modern America,* 2nd ed. (Erlbaum, 2001); full disclosure: my wife, Carol Dana Lanham, contributed an essay to this collection. James A. Berlin's *Writing Instruction in Nineteenth-Century American Colleges* (Southern Illinois University Press, 1984) provides an excellent concise discussion of the debates which set the stage for contemporary composition instruction in America. In his *Rhetoric and Reality: Writing Instruction in American Colleges, 1900–1985* (Southern Illinois University Press, 1987), he brings the story into our own time. These two books together provide an excellent starting point for anyone interested in the general history of writing instruction in America. Courses in prose style itself, remarkably, figure almost nowhere in his accounts.

The difficulties and opportunities for composition in an age of open admissions are admirably illustrated by two books: Mina Shaughnessy's *Errors and Expectations: A Guide for the Teacher of Basic Writing* (Oxford University Press, 1977); and, more recently, Mike Rose's excellent collection of essays, *An Open Language: Selected Writings on Literacy, Learning, and Opportunity* (Bedford/St. Martin's, 2006). The difficulties of writing program administration today are described in Sharon James McGee and Carolyn Handa, eds., *Discord and Direction: The Postmodern Writing Program Administrator* (Utah State University Press, 2005).

Freshman Composition texts continue to multiply beyond enumeration. Readers interested in their development —or lack of it—might compare a sampling of current texts with earlier ones. For the language in our national life, the beginning study is Noah Webster, *Dissertations on the English Language* (1789; Scholars' Facsimiles & Reprints, with an introduction by Harry R. Warfel, 1951). The most complete, and in many ways the most thoughtful, nineteenth-century text is Alexander Bain's *English Composition and Rhetoric* (2 vols., American Book Co., 1888). Bain is especially thorough on the emotional effects of verbal ornamentation.

The current form of The Books seems to have come of age around 1900. See, as varied examples: Austin Phelps and Henry Allyn Frink, *Rhetoric: Its Theory and Practice* (C. Scribner's Sons, 1895); George Herbert Palmer, *Self-Cultivation in English*—this little tract really does return you to yesteryear —(Houghton Mifflin, 1897); J. B. Wisely, *A New English Grammar* (Inland, 1898); John Franklin Genung, *The Working Principles of Rhetoric* (Ginn, 1900).

As for twentieth-century textbooks, perhaps a representative sampling may serve as starting point for further investigation. They offer varied approaches and pleasures to which the reader may feel that I have not always done justice here. Cobbett's *English Grammar,* in the form of letters to his son, for example, strains the epistolary form to its utmost but creates a kind of humor in doing it. And Johnson and Hartley's *Written Composition in American Colleges* offers an example of the kind of educational testing which seems, to me at least, as far off the right track as it is possible to go. Genung's *Working Principles of Rhetoric* mentioned above, on the other hand, has a chapter on rhythm in prose and poetry comparable books seldom have and usually need. Leonard's *English Composition as a Social Problem* is a guide to teaching writing in secondary school, and representative of the attitudes common at that level, attitudes which have continually floated up to post-secondary instruction.

James Bradstreet Greenough and George Lyman Kittredge, *Words and Their Ways in English Speech* (Macmillan, 1901)

Robert Waters, *The English Grammar of William Cobbett, in a series of letters addressed to his son* (Peter Eckler, 1901)

Hammond Lamont, *English Composition* (Scribner, 1906)

Robert Herrick and Lindsay Todd Damon. *Composition and Rhetoric, for Schools* (Scott, Foresman, 1908)

Sterling Andrus Leonard, *English Composition as a Social Problem* (Houghton Mifflin, 1917)

H. Robinson Shipherd, *The Fine Art of Writing, for Those Who Teach It* (Macmillan, 1926)

Burges Johnson and Helene Hartley, *Written Composition in American Colleges* (Union College, 1936)

Harold F. Graves, *Types of Persuasion* (Cordon, 1938)

Donald Davidson, *American Composition and Rhetoric* (Scribner, 1939)

John C. Hodges, *Harbrace College Handbook* (Harcourt Brace, 1941)

Cleanth Brooks and Robert Penn Warren, *Modern Rhetoric* (Harcourt Brace, 1949)

James M. McCrimmon, *Writing with a Purpose* (Houghton Mifflin, 1950)

George S. Wykoff and Harry Shaw, *The Harper Handbook of College Composition* (Harper, 1952)

Donald J. Lloyd and Harry R. Warfel, *American English in Its Cultural Setting* (Knopf, 1957)

Harold C. Martin, *The Logic and Rhetoric of Exposition* (Rinehart, 1958)

Richard E. Hughes and P. Albert Duhamel, *Rhetoric, Principles and Usage* (Prentice-Hall, 1962)

Edward P. J. Corbett, *Classical Rhetoric for the Modern Student* (Oxford, 1965)

Sheridan Baker, *The Complete Stylist* (Crowell, 1966)

John M. Kierzek and Walter Gibson, *The Macmillan Handbook of English* (Macmillan, 1966)

Robert W. Daniel, *A Contemporary Rhetoric* (Little, Brown, 1967)

William Schwab, *Guide to Modern Grammar and Exposition* (Harper & Row, 1967)

Alan H. Vrooman, *Good Writing: An Informal Manual of Style* (Atheneum, 1967)

Richard M. Eastman, *Style* (Oxford, 1970)

Roger Sale, *On Writing* (Random House, 1970)

Virginia Tufte, *Grammar as Style* (Holt, Rinehart and Winston, 1971)

James E. Miller, Jr., *Word, Self, Reality* (Dodd, Mead, 1972)

Rudolf Flesch, *Say What You Mean* (Harper & Row, 1973)

Peter Richardson, *Style: A Pragmatic Approach* (Allyn and Bacon, 1998)

The best of "The Books" since the first edition of this book is Frederick Crews, *The Random House Handbook* (various editions and dates). A shorter but excellent textbook is Joseph M. Williams's *Style: Ten Lessons in Clarity and Grace,* 2nd ed. (Scott, Foresman, 1985).

For more scholarly discussions of prose style, see J. Middleton Murry, *The Problem of Style* (Oxford, 1922); Bonamy Dobree, *Modern Prose Style* (Oxford, 1937); James R. Sutherland, *On English Prose* (University of Toronto Press, 1957); Herbert Read, *English Prose Style* (Bell, 1928). Murry is much the most thoughtful of the four, but all preach the gospel of normative clarity. A more recent survey of style and recent thinking about it is Graham Hough's *Style and Stylistics* (Routledge & Kegan Paul, 1969), a sensible and commendably brief introduction to the current study of style. My *Analyzing Prose,* 2nd ed. (Continuum, 2003), discusses the basic English prose styles. A longer and more ambitious book is James L. Kinneavy's *A Theory of Discourse* (Prentice-Hall, 1971). In setting forth his theory, Kinneavy surveys practically every other theory, classical and modern. His bibliographies are especially useful.

Longer bibliographies, especially of more recent stylistic study, are: Richard W. Bailey and Dolores M. Burton, *English Stylistics: A Bibliography* (MIT Press, 1967); Louis T. Milic, *Style and Stylistics: An Analytical Bibliography* (Free Press, 1967). Finally, Virginia Postrel has written an excellent broad survey of style in modern culture, *The Substance of Style* (HarperCollins, 2003).

On the pedagogy of style, Jacques Barzun has many sensible things to say in *Teacher in America* (Little, Brown, 1945). On the place of stylistic study in modern pedagogy, readers following the standard pedagogy bibliographies might not come across the recurrent excellent discussions in Alfred North Whitehead's *The Aims of Education* (Macmillan, 1929). Many of the philosophical and pedagogical problems touched on in the foregoing chapters received their first full modern discussion in John Henry Cardinal Newman's *The Idea of a University* (1853–58). An interesting study by a political scientist, Robert F. Lane, *The Liberties of Wit* (Yale University Press, 1961), considers the civic consequences of the literary emphasis on style rather than verifiable conceptual content. A conservative view of the modern academic atmosphere and its implications for stylistic study is presented in Jacques Barzun's *The House of Intellect* (Harper, 1959); a liberal view, in Neil Postman and Charles Weingartner's *Teaching as a Subversive Activity* (Delacorte Press, 1969).

For comprehensive collections of comment on style by both the famous and the forgotten, consult: the collection edited by William T. Brewster, *Representative Essays on the Theory of Style* (Macmillan, 1913); Rollo W. Brown, *The Writer's*

Art, by Those Who Have Practiced It (Harvard University Press, 1921); Louis T. Milic, *Stylists on Style* (Scribner, 1969); Leonard Dean and Kenneth G. Wilson, *Essays on Language and Usage,* 2nd ed. (Oxford University Press, 1963); Howard S. Babb, *Essays in Stylistic Analysis* (Harcourt Brace Jovanovich, 1972). Examples of recent work in the overlapping areas of semantics, linguistics, and literary style can be found in *Style in Language,* ed. Thomas A. Sebeok (MIT Press, 1960); *Literary Style: A Symposium,* ed. Seymour Chatman (Oxford University Press, 1971). An especially interesting collection of papers by a single hand is Stephen Ullmann's *Language and Style* (B. Blackwell, 1964).

Modern defenses of ornament in prose are hard to come by. Thomas De Quincey's "Style" is a nineteenth-century *locus classicus* (reprinted in *Selected Essays on Rhetoric by Thomas De Quincey,* ed. Frederick Burwick [Southern Illinois University Press, 1967]); Walter Pater's "Style" (reprinted in the Brewster collection cited above), and Logan Pearsall Smith's gallant rearguard action, "Fine Writing" (*Society for the Preservation of English,* Tract no. 46 [Oxford University Press, 1936]) both argue the case for ornament. The terms used to catalog verbal ornament are arranged both alphabetically and by type in my *A Handlist of Rhetorical Terms,* 2nd ed. (University of California Press, 1991). Discussion of ornamental style occurs passim under various entries there, and a bibliography of classical and Renaissance rhetorical treatises is included.

The issues raised by the dogma of clarity in prose can be pursued in several directions. I. A. Richards has proposed a tripartite division of language in some ways analogous to the three attitudes distinguished in the previous chapters. See

Principles of Literary Criticism (Harcourt Brace, 1930); *The Philosophy of Rhetoric* (Oxford University Press, 1936); and, with C. K. Ogden, *The Meaning of Meaning* (K. Paul Trench Trubner, 1927). The relationship between scientific and intuitive thinking has been explored by Jerome S. Bruner in *The Process of Education* (Vintage Books, 1960) and *On Knowing* (Harvard University Press, 1960). Thomas S. Kuhn's *The Structure of Scientific Revolutions,* 3rd ed. (University of Chicago Press, 1996), is immensely suggestive for the consideration of prose styles as separate paradigms, closed orientations, or systems of value. His discussion of "inter-paradigm debate" really provides the best model currently available for evaluative comparison of different styles. On the outdated scientific theories underlying the dogma of clarity, see Michael Polanyi's *Personal Knowledge* (University of Chicago Press, 1958). Much of his book considers, though not under this rubric, the stylistic component of scientific knowing.

The role of the perceiver can be followed in a number of directions. Ernst Cassirer built his philosophy of symbolic forms on the conception of language as a symbolic reality, something man both conceives and perceives. Man's reality, he argues in *An Essay on Man* (Yale University Press, 1949), is a symbolic one of his own making, not a preexistent one "out there." Thus one can read his *The Logic of the Humanities* (Yale University Press, 1960) as an attack on the very conception of reality The Books' dogma of clarity is built upon. Owen Barfield attacks this "scientific" conception of reality in *Saving the Appearances* (Faber and Faber, 1957), an astute plea for a kind of knowing that allows man to participate in reality—to create it rather than simply observe it. The implications of such a humanistic or mythical theory of knowledge are treated in J. Bronowski's *Science and Human Values* (J. Messner, 1956). The same author's *The Identity of Man* (Natural History Press, 1965) explores the interrelations of theory of knowledge and theory of self, as well as, in a brilliant chapter titled "The Machinery of Nature," dealing with the imaginative or stylistic ingredient in scientific knowing.

The role of the perceiver in art has been dealt with in E. H. Gombrich's classic *Art and Illusion* (Pantheon Books, 1961), a book that manages to grow from an art history focus into a treatment, first of perception in all art, and then of perception itself. Gombrich shows that what we see depends both on what we expect to see and on the frame we have been taught to see it in and with. His conclusions carry profound implications for normative doctrines of prose style. So, too, does Morse Peckham's exciting study of art in terms of the perceiver's role, *Man's Rage for Chaos* (Chilton Books, 1965). Peckham considers art to be not a class of objects but a pattern of expectations in the reader. Here is a theoretical underpinning for the attitudes toward prose developed in the previous chapters. Peckham's theory of art contends that the dynamic operation worked on the observer is finally not an ordering but a disordering one. Again, the implication would be that a normative theory of prose style no longer possesses any theoretical basis.

The Adelbert Ames II experiments mentioned in Chapter 2 have been widely illustrated. The chair perception experiment, for example, is illustrated in John P. Frisby's *Seeing: Illusion, Brain and Mind* (Oxford University Press, 1979), pp.

24–25. The distorted room experiment is illustrated in R. L. Gregory's *Eye and Brain: the psychology of seeing,* 2nd ed. (McGraw-Hill, 1973, pp. 178–80.

The use of the dramatic metaphor to describe both self and society has been most profoundly argued in our time by Kenneth Burke, especially in *The Philosophy of Literary Form,* 2nd ed. (Louisiana State University Press, 1967) and *Permanence and Change,* 3rd ed. (University of California Press, 1984). His idea of style as essentially a way of seeing, a world view or orientation, rather than something seen through, provides the theoretical basis for any philosophical conception of style in our time. His continual effort to move from verbal style to life style, to avoid the unthinking, neutral descriptions of verbal configurations that have so plagued discussions of style, has opened the way to a great deal of thinking about role-playing by social scientists. Readers interested in the idea of self as role might find the writings of the sociologist Erving Goffman of interest, especially the now classic *The Presentation of Self in Everyday Life* (Doubleday, 1959). Wylie Sypher has written eloquently of *Loss of the Self in Modern Literature and Art* (Vintage Books, 1962). And Charles Fair has explored the relation of the two conceptions of self, social and central, in both a physiological and a historical context, in his pessimistic but persuasive *The Dying Self* (Wesleyan University Press, 1969). The writings of R. D. Laing, too, have explored the dynamics of the self; see especially *The Divided Self* (Tavistock, 1959). Erik H. Erikson's views on the growth of the human personality are set forth in his *Childhood and Society* (rev. ed., W. W. Norton, 1963);

a fascinating historical application is made in *Young Man Luther* (W. W. Norton, 1958). More recent publications in this field are far too numerous to list here.

Readers interested in the concept of play and the aesthetic or game model for motive will find Johan Huizinga's *Homo Ludens* (Routledge & Kegan Paul, 1949) of great interest. For a genetic, rather than a historical, analysis, see Jean Piaget's *Play, Dreams and Imitation in Childhood* (trans. C. Gattegno and F. M. Hodgson, New York, 1951).

J. A. C. Brown has provided a sensibly cynical assessment of the force the media exert upon us in *Techniques of Persuasion* (Penguin Books, 1963). His hard-nosed conclusion is that people are less persuadable than we think. If someone is seriously deluded by the media, there must have been something wrong with him to begin with. A more recent study, James B. Twitchell's *Lead Us Into Temptation: The Triumph of American Materialism* (Columbia University Press, 1999) takes a less sanguine view. The distortions often practiced by the media are entertainingly traced in *It Ain't Necessarily So: How Media Make and Unmake the Scientific Picture of Reality,* by David Murray, Joel Schwartz, and S. Robert Lichter (Rowman and Littlefield, 2001).

Jay David Bolter's *Writing Space* (Erlbaum, 1991) provides a good beginning point for considering electronic text, perhaps the most important development in writing and writing instruction since the first edition of this book. Lev Manovich's *The Language of New Media* (MIT Press, 2001) is another good, heavily theoretical, introduction, but his interest lies in film not written text. Janet H. Murray discusses cyberspace narrative in *Hamlet on the Holodeck* (Free Press, 1997). *The In-*

formation Inferno, a stimulating and acute discussion of how text fares in the imagistic spaces of digital expression was published in 2001 by Designer Books, under the pseudonym of "Whodini." I've discussed the movement from book to screen in *The Electronic Word* (University of Chicago Press, 1993) and *The Economics of Attention* (University of Chicago Press, 2006). The classical scholar James J. O'Donnell takes a broader view of the subject in his excellent *Avatars of the Word: From Papyrus to Cyberspace* (Harvard University Press, 1998).

The most stimulating discussion of the relation of syntax to emotional response remains, it seems to me, the "Lexicon Rhetoricae" section of Kenneth Burke's *Counter-Statement* (3rd ed., University of California Press, 1968). Burke's philosophical discussion of verbal ornament as metaphor for motive in *A Rhetoric of Motives* (University of California Press, 1969) remains, too, the most wide-ranging consideration of the implications of verbal ornament. Of the philosophical implications of the neutral style in prose, Roland Barthes's *Writing Degree Zero* (Beacon Press, 1968) constitutes a provocative modern statement.

I cannot close this survey without at least a short comment about a short book that must be the best-selling, and has certainly been the most praised, book about prose style written in America, William Strunk Jr. and E. B. White's *The Elements of Style* (Macmillan, 1959). It has recently been published in a new edition (2006), with illustrations, to rave reviews. It began life as a collection of "Thou shalts" and "Thou shalt nots" compiled by Strunk, a professor at Cornell. All of us who teach composition have compiled such lists and Strunk's is typical but hardly remarkable. To it, the

New Yorker writer E. B. White appended an "Approach to Style" which summarizes The Books' self-contradictory wisdom. I cannot begin to explain Strunk and White's popularity but must leave it to the reader to measure the book against its fashionable acclaim.

Works Cited in Text

Amis, Kingsley. *Lucky Jim.* London: Penguin Books, 1953.

Beecham, Thomas. *A Mingled Chime.* New York: G. P. Putnam's Sons, 1943.

Behrman, S. N. *Duveen.* New York: Random House, 1952.

Bible. *The New English Bible.* Oxford University Press; Cambridge University Press, 1970.

Blair, Hugh. *Lectures on Rhetoric and Belles Lettres.* Vol. 1. Ed. Harold F. Harding. Carbondale: Southern Illinois Press, 1965.

Bloomfield, Morton. *Essays and Explorations.* Cambridge: Harvard University Press, 1970.

Boorstin, Daniel J. *The Image.* New York: Harper & Row, 1964.

Burke, Kenneth. *Counter-Statement.* 2nd ed. Berkeley: University of California Press, 1968.

Burke, Kenneth. *Permanence and Change.* 3rd ed. Berkeley: University of California Press, 1984.

Cassirer, Ernst. *The Logic of the Humanities.* Trans. Clarence Smith Howe. New Haven: Yale University Press, 1967.

Chandler, Raymond. *Raymond Chandler Speaking.* Ed. Dorothy Gardiner and Kathrine Sorley Walker. Boston: Houghton Mifflin, 1962.

Chapman, John Jay. *Learning and Other Essays.* New York: Moffat Yard, 1910.

Cozzens, James Gould. *By Love Possessed.* New York: Harcourt, Brace, 1957.

Crystal, David. *The Cambridge Encyclopedia of the English Language.* Cambridge: Cambridge University Press, 1995.

Delacroix, Henri. *Le Langage et la Pensée,* 2nd ed. Paris: Librairie Félix Alcan, 1930.

Dryden, John. "Preface to the Fables." In *Selected Works of John Dryden.* Ed. William Frost. New York: Rinehart, 1958.

Erasmus. *De Copia.* Trans. Betty I. Knott. In *Collected Works of Erasmus,* vol. 24 (*Literary and Educational Writings 2.* Ed. Craig R. Thompson. Toronto: University of Toronto Press, 1978.

Fielding, Henry. *Shamela.* Ed. Martin C. Battestin. Boston: Houghton Mifflin, 1961.

Fowler, H. W. *The King's English.* 3rd ed. Oxford: Oxford University Press, 1931.

Fowler, H. W. *Modern English Usage.* Oxford: Oxford University Press, 1937.

Frye, Northrop. *The Well-Tempered Critic.* Bloomington: University of Indiana Press, 1963.

Greville, Charles C. F. *The Greville Memoirs,* v. 5. Ed. Henry Reeve. London: Longmans, Green, 1888.

Hemingway, Ernest. *A Farewell to Arms.* New York: Charles Scribner's Sons, 1953.

Huxley, Aldous. *Words and Their Meanings.* Los Angeles: Ward Richey Press, 1940.

Johnson, Samuel. *Dr. Johnson: Prose and Poetry.* Selected by Mona Wilson. Cambridge: Harvard University Press, 1967.

Jones, Alan Pryce. "Translation and the Americans." *Times Literary Supplement,* Sept. 25, 1970.

Joseph, Sister Miriam. *Shakespeare's Use of the Arts of Language.* Philadelphia: Paul Dry Books, 2005.

Kennan, George F. *Democracy and the Student Left.* Boston: Little, Brown, 1968.

Kitzhaber, Albert R. *Themes, Theories, and Therapy: The Teaching of Writing in College.* New York: McGraw-Hill, 1963.

Lanham, Richard A. *Analyzing Prose.* 2nd ed. London: Continuum, 2003.

Lanham, Richard A. *The Economics of Attention.* Chicago: University of Chicago Press, 2006.

Lanham, Richard A. *The Electronic Word.* Chicago: University of Chicago Press, 1993.

Lanham, Richard A. *Revising Prose.* 5th ed. New York: Pearson/Longman, 2006.

Maugham, W. Somerset. *The Summing Up.* London: William Heinemann, 1938.

Meillet, A. *The Comparative Method in Historical Linguistics.* Trans. G. B. Ford, Jr. Paris: Librairie Champion, 1970.

Mills, C. Wright. *The Sociological Imagination.* New York: Oxford University Press, 1959.

Moore, Geoffrey. "American Prose Today." In *Essays on Language and Usage,* ed. Leonard Dean and Kenneth Wilson, 337–354. 2nd ed. New York: Oxford University Press, 1963.

Murry, John Middleton. *The Problem of Style.* Oxford: Oxford University Press, 1922.

Nabokov, Vladimir. *Ada.* Greenwich, Conn.: Fawcett, 1970.

Peckham, Morse. *Man's Rage for Chaos.* Philadelphia: Chilton Books, 1965.

Pope, Alexander. *Selected Poetry and Prose.* Ed. William K. Wimsatt. 2nd ed. New York: Holt, Rinehart and Winston, 1972.

Read, Herbert. *English Prose Style.* London: Bell, 1928.

Roberts, Paul. "The Relation of Linguistics to the Teaching of English." *College English,* October, 1960.

Saintsbury, George. *A History of English Prose Rhythm.* Westport, Conn.: Greenwood Press, 1978.

Sebeok, T. A. *Style in Language.* Cambridge: MIT Press, 1960.

Shipherd, H. Robinson. *The Fine Art of Writing.* New York: Macmillan, 1926.

Sledge, E. B. *With the Old Breed, at Peleliu and Okinawa.* Intro. Paul Fussell. New York: Oxford University Press, 1990.

Stigler, George J. *The Intellectual and the Marketplace.* Cambridge: Harvard University Press, 1984.

Sutherland, James R. *On English Prose.* Toronto: University of Toronto Press, 1957.

Whatmough, Joshua. *Language.* New York: St. Martin's Press, 1956.

Wimsatt, W. K. *The Prose Style of Samuel Johnson.* New Haven: Yale University Press, 1941.

Woolf, Virginia. *To the Lighthouse.* New York: Harcourt Brace, 1927.

Yablonsky, Lewis. *The Hippie Trip.* New York: Pegasus, 1968.

Printed in the USA
CPSIA information can be obtained
at www.ICGtesting.com
JSHW081241160224
57502JS00001B/2

9 781589 880320